1979

On the Verge of Revolt

ON THE VERGE OF REVOLT

Women in American Films of the Fifties

Brandon French

FREDERICK UNGAR PUBLISHING CO.   *New York*

Copyright © 1978 by Frederick Ungar Publishing Co., Inc.
Printed in the United States of America
Designed by Jacqueline Schuman

Library of Congress Cataloging in Publication Data

French, Brandon, 1944–
    On the verge of revolt.

    Bibliography: p.
    Includes index.
    1. Women in moving-pictures. 2. Moving-pictures
—United States. I. Title.
PN1995.9.W6F7   791.43′0909′352   78–4294
ISBN 0–8044–2220–6
ISBN 0–8044–6158–9 pbk.

For Stephen Booth

Acknowledgments

I wish to thank three people in particular for helping me complete this book: Ramona Pearson, who generously provided me with a way to view virtually all the films of the fifties which I requested, and introduced me to others I had not thought to see; Alan Chapman, who shamed me in the margins of every page by pointing out spelling mistakes, errors in logic, and baroque syntax; and Stan Hochman, my editor, who adamantly held out for a better book.

It was as if the whole period of the fifties was a front, the topsoil that protected the seed of rebellion that was germinating below.

Molly Haskell
From Reverence to Rape

Contents

Introduction:
The Transitional Woman

The Western myth of world order is based upon a hierarchy of male dominance descending from God the Father. The Bible says, "But I would have you know, that the head of every man is Christ: and the head of woman is man; and the head of Christ is God" (Corinthians I, ch. 2). During the 1960s, this notion of male supremacy was challenged for the second time in the history of America by an outbreak of militant feminism. Much like the first outbreak in the nineteenth century—which began officially in 1848 at the first women's rights convention, held in Seneca Falls, New York, and culminated in 1920 in the ratification of the 19th amendment of the Constitution, granting women the right to vote—the *new* feminism arose as a reaction against repression in the form of a sentimental glorification of marriage, motherhood, and homemaking as the definitive parameters of womanhood.

But even though this second feminist revolt might have been anticipated, it was so inconsistent with the *predominant* attitudes of the culture that it appeared to combust spontaneously, without any clear origin. As the historian Lois W. Banner writes, "In the face of the virulent antifeminism of American society in the immediate post-war years and the strong appeal of domesticity in the 1950s, the rise of a militant feminism in the 1960s is surprising." [1] The women whom Merle Miller attacked in *Esquire* (1954) as an "increasing and strident minority . . . who are doing their damnedest to wreck marriage and homelife in America . . . who insist on having both a husband and a career" [2] were not sufficiently strident to invade the conscious-

---

[1] *Women in Modern America: A Brief History* (New York: Harcourt, Brace, 1974).
[2] Douglas T. Miller and Marion Nowak, *The Fifties: The Way We Really Were* (Garden City, New York: Doubleday, 1977).

ness of the culture and shake its collective conviction that domestic harmony was a function of wholesale female retreat to the home. The fact that in the fifties, "more than one-third of the working women [in America] were shouldering the responsibilities for a home and children of school age along with an outside job," that by 1955, "the proportion of women in the work force exceeded the highest level reached during the war," and that "between 1940 and 1960 the number of working wives doubled and the number of working mothers quadrupled," [3] became lost beneath the image of the woman-as-homemaker which the fifties projected upon the female sex. The following statements made in 1955, in the course of a United Auto Workers Union debate, suggest the nature of this paradoxical situation:

> Delegate Chantres, Local 600: . . . If you will look closely at the resolution all that is asked in this resolution is job security for women workers. . . . Job security for women workers does not mean whether they should work or not. They already have been working in the plants for years and years, and all they want now is job security as the men have today, like seniority. . . .
>
> By the way, I want to inject this before anyone believes that my wife is working. My wife is not working; she is taking care of three kids. Incidentally, I am one of those people that is opposed to women working. . . .
> President Reuther: . . . I come from a family that, thank God, had a mother who stayed home and took care of her children. But there are good mothers and bad mothers, and there are good fathers and bad fathers.
>
> What we are talking about is if a woman is working whether we are going to protect her rights. . . .[4]

In a similar act of simultaneous acknowledgment and denial, the blissful picture of familial felicity—the happy housewife—was not

---

[3] Mary P. Ryan, *Womanhood in America: From Colonial Times to the Present* (New York: Harper & Row, 1975).
[4] "A union protects its women members: *United Auto Workers (1955),*" *The Female Experience: An American Documentary,* ed. Gerda Lerner (Indianapolis: Bobbs-Merrill, 1977).

challenged by her growing susceptibility to what came to be called "the housewife's syndrome," a "terrible tiredness [that] took . . . many women to doctors in the 1950's. . . ." [5] A psychiatrist of that decade would have instructed these women to stop fighting and adjust to their feminine destiny; he might have prescribed an afternoon each week away from home, or at the most, a part-time job; that is, a little escape so that there would be no real escape from their domestic duties, no major disruption or reconception of their female role.[6]

According to Alexander Lowen in *The Betrayal of the Body* (London: Collier Books, 1969), alienation from a disturbing reality (such as women's emancipation), followed by the replacement of reality with an idealized image (such as "the happy housewife"), is schizoid:

> The schizoid disturbance creates a dissociation of the image from reality. . . . An image derives its reality from its association with feeling or sensation. When this association is disrupted, the image becomes abstract. The discrepancy between image and reality is most clearly seen in delusional schizophrenics. . . . On the other hand, "mental health" refers to the condition where image and reality coincide.

Schizoid denial is a defense against terror and catastrophe. Lowen writes, "If the denial is complete, the terror vanishes." The denial of the fifties, however, was not complete, and America's terror surfaced in a variety of guises: not only in the compulsive whitewash of women's emancipation, but in the hysteria of McCarthyism, the obsession with nuclear annihilation, and the rabid overreaction to any violation of middle-class decorum, from singer Elvis Presley to "beatnik" poet Allen Ginsberg. Women's emancipation, however, posed the most immediate threat to the American way of life, as well as a buried threat to the basic tenet of world order, male supremacy. As playwright August Strindberg wrote at the turn of the century, "I, for my part, could foresee all the results of this woman's movement. To depose man and put woman in his place . . . to dethrone the true

---

[5] Betty Friedan, *The Feminine Mystique* (New York: Dell, 1963).
[6] This description of a solution to "the housewife's syndrome" is derived from "A Modern Housewife's Lament: Herma L. Snider (1960)," *The Female Experience,* ed. Gerda Lerner.

lords of the world who created civilization . . . a direct challenge to my sex." [7]

The emancipation of thé fifties gained its impetus from the industrial boom that accompanied America's entrance into World War II, a situation that permitted women to temporarily replace men.

> . . . no less than 8 million women entered the work force during World War II. . . . Females could now be found in such novel places as on the docks, in the steel mills, behind the steering wheels in cabs and buses. American airlines employed hundreds of women, not merely as stewardesses, but as pilots and mechanics.[8]

Women's change of status is reflected in American films of the forties. Before 1941, women characters who work in movies usually do so "in sectors of the economy carved out almost exclusively for their sex . . . [as] nurses, school teachers, librarians . . . social workers," [9] secretaries and an occasional artist and junior editor. For example, Saunders (Jean Arthur), the clever woman in *Mr. Smith Goes to Washington* (1939), who shows Jefferson Smith the senatorial ropes and ultimately saves his hide, is only a secretary.

But after 1941, women in movies begin to do "man-sized" jobs. In *Woman of the Year* (1941), Katharine Hepburn plays a celebrated political journalist; in *Lady in the Dark* (1944), Ginger Rogers is a magazine editor; Ingrid Bergman portrays a psychiatrist who cures a psychotic patient in *Spellbound* (1945); Joan Crawford evolves from a housewife to the owner of a chain of successful Southern California restaurants in *Mildred Pierce* (1945); Jean Arthur is a congresswoman in *A Foreign Affair* (1948); and in *Adam's Rib* (1949), Katharine Hepburn plays a lawyer who successfully defends a dazed housewife accused of attempting to murder her husband and his mistress.

---

[7] "The Vampire Wife," *Masculine/Feminine: Readings in Sexual Mythology and the Liberation of Women,* ed. Betty Roszak and Theodore Roszak (New York: Harper & Row, 1969). From *A Madman's Defense (Le Plaidoyer d'un Fou),* tr. and ed. Evert Sprinchorn (New York: Doubleday, 1967).
[8] Mary P. Ryan, *Womanhood in America.*
[9] *ibid.*

In real life, however, as soon as the war ended, more than two million women were ousted from the working world as American men returned home to reclaim their civilian jobs, although a Woman's Bureau Study conducted in 1944 indicated that 80 percent of the women who were employed during World War II wanted to continue in their jobs after the war ended. But after a brief hiatus, the expanded production of the postwar economy made it incumbent upon business and industry to permit women to re-enter the work force, although no longer in the jobs reserved for men nor at salaries equivalent to those of men. In the meantime, they also married and embarked upon the creation of the postwar baby boom. In other words, women on a mass scale began to lead a double life.

It was double, rather than full, because women were encouraged by the culture to dissociate their identities from their jobs; encouraged, that is, to adopt the culture's schizoid dislocation by defining themselves entirely through their roles as wives, mothers, and homemakers, regardless of what else they did:

> Without quite realizing it, we have come to depend on a work force of married women who do not think of themselves as workers and are not treated seriously on the job. Only when we look back into history do we see how they have been pulled into wage work and pushed back home at the convenience of the changing economy.[10]

The domestic female image that dominated the reality of the late forties and the fifties was the product of certain sociologists, psychologists, anthropologists, educators, authors, and physicians,[11] as well as the organs of mass media, which preached the dangers of women's lost femininity and the bounties which awaited women within the

[10] Caroline Bird, *Born Female: The High Cost of Keeping Women Down* (New York: Pocket Books, 1969).
[11] Author Philip Wylie (*Generation of Vipers*, 1942); Freudian psychoanalyst Helene Deutsch (*The Psychology of Women*, 1944); Dr. Benjamin Spock (*Baby and Childcare*, 1946); sociologists Farnham and Lundberg (*Modern Woman: The Lost Sex*, 1947); anthropologist Margaret Mead; and educator Lynn White are some of the names that recur in most discussions of the cultural influences on women in the forties. See Betty Friedan, *The Feminine Mystique*, chapters 5–7, for the fullest discussion of these influences.

boundaries of the traditional female role. It coexisted throughout the forties with a more emancipated female image; oftentimes, the two images were combined to create a double message. Films such as *Woman of the Year* and *Mildred Pierce,* for example, depict women in positions of unprecedented power and authority, but both films discredit their heroines as bad wives and indifferent, or overambitious, mothers, and each movie ends with its heroine's renunciation of ambitions in favor of a static domesticity:

> . . . the antifeminism of the post-war 1940s held women responsible for society's ills—either because they were failures as mothers or because they had left the home for work.[12]

Other more rabidly paranoid films, such as *The Maltese Falcon* (1941), *Double Indemnity* (1944), *The Postman Always Rings Twice* (1946), and *Gun Crazy* (1949), portray ambitious women as craven monsters, emotionless killers who seduce men into their evil service and who must be destroyed like mad dogs.

It is naive, however, to assume that movies, or mass media in general, whether television and advertising or the attitudes expressed in books and articles, could have turned the tide of the culture in a predominantly conservative direction unless the vast majority of Americans were receptive to these reactionary messages. The reform spirit as a whole, of which women's emancipation was only a part, fell into disrepute and atrophied in the decade that followed the war. Life, which had been disrupted both by the Depression, and then by the war, at last seemed destined to resume a "normal" course, and although this destiny was not fulfilled, except in terms of economic prosperity, American sentiment clung to the hope and ignored, denied, or attempted to redefine any contrary evidence—even the Korean War. "We are not at war," President Truman told the American public in 1950. ". . . the United States was trying to suppress 'a bandit raid' on the Republic of Korea." [13]

---

[12] Lois W. Banner, *Women in Modern America: A Brief History.*
[13] Eric F. Goldman, *The Crucial Decade—And After: America 1945–1960* (New York: Random House, 1960).

The movie which best reflects America's state of mind as it made the transition from war to peace in the late forties is William Wyler's *The Best Years of Our Lives* (1947). Among other things, the film dramatizes the conviction of its three male protagonists that *women* must provide what the government and business did not, to repay them for sacrificing the best years of their lives:

> A new definition of the family was constructed out of an absorption of all emotional satisfaction into the home. . . . The domestic unit was an emotional refuge in a bureaucratized and routinized society.[14]

This expectation of women is exemplified, in part, by the film's comparison of two female characters, Marie (Virginia Mayo) and Peggy (Teresa Wright). Marie is the wife of one of the three protagonists, Fred Derry (Dana Andrews). When Derry returns home from the war, his wife is working—at a nightclub. (All the other women in the film are home when their men return, even though some have held jobs.) Derry spends the night at the apartment of one of the other protagonists, Al (Fredric March), and meets Al's daughter, Peggy. When Derry, a former officer in the Air Force, awakens in the middle of the night, hysterical from a recurrent nightmare about the death of one of his men, Peggy comforts him, passing her hand over his face to erase the painful past. Derry is reunited with his wife the next day and although she is glad to see him, she resents his insistence that she quit her job in the nightclub. Her resentment increases when she must play the good homemaker while Fred, unable to find a decent job, is forced to resume his old life—without status, and with only a subsistence wage—as a clerk and soda jerk in a drug store. Marie wants to have fun, and has the audacity to expect married life to be more than drudgery. Although she is willing to share the financial responsibility of the marriage by working, she is treated in the film as childish and something of a whore (Fred eventually catches her with another man). By failing to fulfill Fred's expectations, Marie

---

14 Mary P. Ryan, *Womanhood in America*. This notion is derived from Talcott Parsons and Robert Bales, *Family, Socialization and Interaction Process* (1955).

becomes the symbol of Fred's disappointment in America as a whole.

But Peggy reverses his despair. For, she is substantial and nurturing, a virginal mother image who offers unconditional love. When she and Fred are finally united at the end of the film, and Fred describes the hardship they will have to endure before he "makes it," the camera holds on a rapturous close-up of Peggy's face, her eyes shining, her mouth trembling with self-sacrificial love.

The movie even suggests that homemaking can be the postwar foundation of economic, as well as emotional, sustenance, when Fred eventually finds work converting his beloved bomber planes into prefabricated houses, the literalization of turning swords into plowshares, making construction from destruction. Thus, the idea of the woman-centered home comes to represent a large part of the film's optimism, that which is shored up against the nightmare of the past, and the international chaos and national indifference of the present: "the happy family huddling together against the visceral terror of modern times." [15]

The terror in *The Best Years of Our Lives* is clearly male rather than female. But there was real life female terror, as well, which went unrecorded: the terror of independence, freedom, self-reliance, success.[16] Women in the forties may have been able to do "a man's job," but they had no psychological preparation for participating in men's mythic roles as rulers of the earth, designers of destiny, and heads of the family—those heady, dreadful responsibilities, that awesome power. The character Elena in Norman Mailer's novel *The Deerpark* (1955) perfectly captures many women's ambivalence about their first taste of autonomy, and their subsequent retreat to the primitive biological role they had been socialized to perceive as their unique destiny:

---

[15] Miller and Nowak, *The Fifties: The Way We Really Were.*

[16] In the late sixties, psychologist Matina Horner discovered that over 80 percent of the college women she studied had "a deep seated resistance to worldly achievement" which she called "fear of success." (Mary P. Ryan, *Womanhood in America,* derived from Vivian Gornick, "Why Radcliffe Women Are Afraid of Success," *The New York Times Magazine,* January 14, 1973.)

> Yes, Charley. As of now I am free and it's frightening. Oh, Charley boy, it's terrifying as hell. Because women, Charley, weren't born to be free, they were born to have babies, I suppose, and I am getting weird and wild and really scared inside, because it's too good, Charley . . .

Elena eventually fulfills her "female destiny," marrying Charley and becoming a mother, yet her last appearance in the novel takes the form of a desperate question:

> . . . what I'm trying to say is, I mean, we have the baby, and we'll probably have another baby, and I have good relations with the servants and I do love the dancing classes, and Charley, I love you, I can tell because I still get scared at the thought of losing you, but Charley, listen to me, I don't know if you understand how much I love Vickie [their son], I keep worrying that I won't be a good enough mother to him, but is that enough? Is Vickie enough? I mean where do I go? I don't want to complain, but what am I going to do with my life?

A female character in James Jones's fifties novel *From Here to Eternity* asks essentially the same question. But in films of the fifties (including the film of *From Here to Eternity*), such a question was almost never asked. Nonetheless, movies of that decade recorded American women's dissatisfaction and tentative rebellion with a surprising degree of fidelity. They did it in such a way, however, that virtually no one noticed.

On the surface, fifties films promoted women's domesticity and inequality and sought easy, optimistic conclusions to any problems their fictions treated. But a significant number of movies simultaneously reflected, unconsciously or otherwise, the malaise of domesticity and the untenably narrow boundaries of the female role. By providing a double text, which contradicted itself without acknowledging any contradiction—that is, by imitating the culture's schizoid "doublethink"—they documented the practical, sexual, and emotional transition women were undergoing beneath the threshold of the contemporary audience's conscious awareness.

The most overt, but less radical, evidence of women's transition toward a raised consciousness occurs in films of the early fifties (1950–1952). In these films, women openly assert their equality, even their superiority, in relation to the men they love. But they do not, for the most part, challenge their destinies as wives and mothers or lovers.

In films made from 1953 to 1956, the most politically reactionary and socially conformist phase of the fifties, women's unhappiness is treated not as a measure of enforced inequality or relegation to an oppressed role, but of loneliness and sexual starvation. The acknowledgment of women's sexual needs, and the concomitant escape from the sexual double standard, is an advance. But the films reveal how sex and love were often misused to obscure or resolve deeper sources of female (and male) dissatisfaction.

From 1957 to 1959, certain films harbor evidence of *radical* transition, in men as well as women, but the revolutionary content is heavily camouflaged. The reassertion of women's equality, the commitment to career over marriage, and the renunciation of marriage as a male-dominated institution which demands an impossible degree of obedience, are hidden beneath the habit of nuns. The substitution of androgyny for rigid male and female roles is reassuringly cloaked in comedy or farce.

On the Verge of Revolt presents close analyses of thirteen films drawn from these three phases of the fifties: *Sunset Boulevard* (1950), *The Quiet Man* (1952), and *The Marrying Kind* (1952); *Shane* (1953), *From Here to Eternity* (1953), *The Country Girl* (1955), *The Tender Trap* (1955), *Marty* (1955), *All that Heaven Allows* (1956), and *Picnic* (1956); *Heaven Knows, Mr. Allyson* (1957), *The Nun's Story* (1958), and *Some Like It Hot* (1959). Peripheral attention is also paid to *Adam's Rib* (1949), *The African Queen* (1950), *The Big Heat* (1952), *The Shrike* (1955), *The Seven Year Itch* (1957), *The Misfits* (1959), *Auntie Mame* (1959), and *Psycho* (1960), among others.

I selected these particular films because each sheds light on a different cluster of issues and situations women faced in their transition from the forties to the sixties: romance, courtship, work, marriage, sex, motherhood, divorce, loneliness, adultery, alcoholism, widowhood, heroism, madness, and ambition. Most of these films also offer insight into *men's* transition during the same period, thereby providing a picture of how men and women affected one another's growth.

But these movies are by no means the only financially successful or critically acclaimed movies I might have chosen to illustrate the sexual transitions of the fifties. For example, in *The Greatest Show on Earth* (1952), the Betty Hutton character competes for the center ring in the circus against a male trapeze artist and, in her excellence, drives him to take a risk which results in a crippling accident. In contrast, the lover in *Dangerous When Wet* (1953) provides moral support for the Esther Williams character as she swims the English Channel for money to save her family's farm; he swims alongside her for the last stretch to reassure her that she has the stamina to win the competition. In *The Court Jester* (1956), Glynis Johns portrays a revolutionary powerhouse who arranges and leads an insurrection, clubs the film's villain, and teaches her boyfriend, played by Danny Kaye, that manhood can be tender and gentle. Natalie Wood delivers the same message to James Dean in *Rebel Without a Cause* (1955). In *Peyton Place* (1957), a young woman (Hope Lange) is raped by her stepfather and later kills him in self-defense when he attempts a second violation. In the same film, another young woman (Diane Varsi) tells her boyfriend (Russ Tamblyn), "It's about time you learned that girls want to do the same things as boys." Finally, in *Pillowtalk* (1959), Doris Day plays a successful interior decorator who bitterly satirizes her boyfriend's compulsive promiscuity by turning his apartment into a sultan's seraglio, thereby confronting him with the real nature of his attitude toward women.

These movies, like the ones analyzed in the chapters that follow, are a mixture of progressive and reactionary elements. For transition is a time of conflict and contradiction, as well as growth and change. When stable patterns break down, both old and new alternatives compete for ascendancy. The transitional woman is often torn between her desire for a conventional, secure lifestyle and her longing for an unconventional, adventurous, largely uncharted course of action. Or she may exhibit two contradictory modes of behavior, stemming from confusion about her real nature and her traditional female role. These conflicts and contradictions, as much as the positive advances, are signs of life in what has hitherto been dismissed as a moribund, conformist, counterrevolutionary decade. They are the gathering thunder of revolt that an entire culture chose not to hear, or hearing, failed to comprehend.

1

The Scarlet "A"

Sunset Boulevard *(1950)*

*What such stories hardly ever manage to show us is a legitimate,
human, orderly ambition, a decent, sporting desire to be the best at
something. The suggestion, plainly, is that such a temperate project
will get you nowhere, because it won't make you a killer, and if
you're not a killer, you won't win.*

Michael Wood, America in the Movies *(1975)*

Sunset Boulevard is a film about ambition, and what it allegedly
does to the human spirit. I say "allegedly" because it is next to impossible for an American to be objective about ambition. On the one
hand, we are baptized in the sprightly wisdom of Horatio Alger that
success could and should be ours if we have sufficient drive, spunk,
push, and, to borrow a neologism from Walt Disney, "stick-to-it-
tivity." On the other hand, we harbor a gloomy suspicion that ambition
corrodes the soul.

America's negative attitude toward ambition had a critical in-
fluence on the transitional woman of the fifties. An ambitious woman
not merely violated the domestic female image; she became a recep-
tacle for America's most distorted fantasy projections about ambition:
a soulless monster of selfish manipulation without moral restraint,

1

like Mr. Kurtz in Joseph Conrad's novella *The Heart of Darkness*. This fantasy of the female materialized throughout the forties and early fifties in the movie genre called *film noir*.

Billy Wilder's *Sunset Boulevard*, an example of late *film noir*, characterizes ambition as deadly, the scarlet "A" of our twentieth-century puritan conscience. And like other *film noir* movies, *Sunset Boulevard* depicts a woman who is more ambitious than the man she covets, calling up the biblical image of a fallen Eve seducing Adam into sin.

However, Norma Desmond, the middle-aged has-been movie queen who seduces and ultimately kills a luckless screenwriter, is not a typically enigmatic "just plain rotten" *film noir* villainess. Nor is Betty Scheafer, with whom the screenwriter falls in love, simply a sweet young contrast to Norma. And Joe Gillis, the object of both women's desires, is not merely an innocent victim. Because Wilder complicates the *film noir* formula of evil woman–naive man–innocent ingenue, his film provides insight into the emotional ambivalence of transitional women in the fifties.

Sunset Boulevard begins at the end, as Norma (Gloria Swanson) fires three shots. Joe (William Holden), mortally wounded, staggers toward Norma's pool and falls into it. As we stare up at his spread-eagle corpse, floating with open eyes on the surface of the water, Gillis, in an extended pun on the word "ghostwriter," begins to narrate the events which led to his demise.

The scene shifts to workaday Hollywood where Joe tries to sell an idea for a movie to a Paramount Studios producer. But Betty (Nancy Olson), one of the studio readers, delivers a devastating denunciation of Joe's screenplay treatment, so the producer turns him down.

Later, on the lam from two "finance boys" who want to repossess his car, Joe has a blowout and pulls into the Sunset Boulevard driveway of "one of those great big houses in the ten thousand block." There he is mistaken for an undertaker and escorted into the house by an ominous German butler named Max (Erich von Stroheim). The mistress of the mansion, Norma, asks him to provide a coffin for her dead monkey.

When Joe reveals his actual identity, Norma is indignant, then intrigued. Her rough draft of a screenplay, "Salome," needs to be rewritten as a vehicle for her comeback (her "return," as she calls it, "to the millions of people who've never forgiven me for deserting the screen"). Joe—without job, car, or money—agrees to take on the assignment and is moved by Max into an apartment above the garage of the mansion.

Norma falls in love with Joe, lavishing clothes and gifts upon him. Later, when the apartment roof leaks in a rainstorm, Joe is transferred into the main house and set up in "the room of the husband. Of the husbands, I should say," Max explains. "Madame has been married three times."

During a bizarre New Year's Eve party, Norma confesses her passion for Joe, causing him to walk out. He turns up at a Hollywood party given by his assistant director friend Artie Green (Jack Webb), "as nice a guy as ever lived." There he reencounters Betty, who we learn is Artie's girl friend. Joe and Betty discuss an idea for a screenplay that they might write together.

When Joe calls Max to request that his things be sent over to Artie's place, Max tells him that "Madame" has attempted suicide. Joe returns to the Sunset Boulevard mansion and out of pity and guilt ("You're the only person in this stinking town that has been good to me") becomes Norma's lover.

Norma sends her rewritten screenplay to Cecil B. DeMille and waits happily for his response. Through a misunderstanding, she is prompted to visit DeMille (who plays himself in the movie) at Paramount. He gives her a gentle brush-off, but she misinterprets his response and returns home to begin a slavish beauty regimen that will restore her to star condition.

Joe sneaks off at night in the Desmond limousine to Paramount where he meets Betty to work on their screenplay. They fall in love, and Norma becomes pathologically suspicious.

When Joe returns to the mansion one evening, he discovers Norma on the phone with Betty, telling her where (and how) Joe lives. Joe grabs the phone and invites Betty to come see for herself. Betty arrives in the middle of the night and after seeing Joe's predicament, asks him to leave with her. He refuses, she leaves, and he begins to pack, ready to quit Hollywood entirely and return to Dayton, Ohio, where he was once a newspaper copy editor.

Norma takes a gun she had purchased to kill herself and in a repetition of the first scene of the film shoots Joe instead.

In the final sequence, newsmen are gathered in the mansion awaiting Norma's surrender to the police. Norma, quite mad by now, assumes (with Max's encouragement) that the press gathering heralds the advent of her longed-for return. As she descends the stairway of her mansion, Max directs the news cameras to roll. Norma moves sinuously into an awesome close-up, staring directly at the audience, "all those wonderful people out there in the dark." Fate has intervened to provide Norma with a perverse fulfillment of her dream.

According to Phyllis Chesler in *Women and Madness* (1972), women tend to turn their aggression inward, onto themselves, in the form of masochism and suicide. Norma's suicide attempts are so numerous that all the locks have been removed from the doors in her mansion to abet her rescue. But at the end of *Sunset Boulevard,* Norma finally manages to turn her aggression outward, onto someone else; and in a dreadful sense, that is a triumph, just as her brief comeback before the newsreel cameras is a victory, however feeble and ironic.

In shooting Joe, Norma—like Miss Havisham in Charles Dickens's *Great Expectations,* to whom she is obliquely compared in Joe's narration—strikes out against the defection of her lover, not merely Joe but what Joe symbolizes to her: the audience who has ceased to love her and thereby robbed her of her only creative outlet. She also gives vent to a thinly disguised fury against all men. For the central irony of Norma's existence as a woman is that she is dependent on men, while at the same time she is the powerhouse who supports them.

Not only does Norma keep Max, whom we learn was at one time her director and her first husband, but also Joe. And as the star of twelve DeMille pictures, "his biggest successes," she asserts her

Sunset Boulevard. Betty (Nancy Olson) and Joe (William Holden) trade romantic platitudes in a bathroom on New Year's Eve. The setting is a subtle comment on the tawdriness of their relationship, since both characters are involved with other people.

claim to a portion of *his* maintenance as well. Nonetheless, she is dependent upon Max to protect her from the reality of her abandonment by the outside world, dependent upon Joe to rewrite her script for her and to love her, and dependent upon DeMille to restore her career in the movies.

Like Clytemnestra, Regan, and Lady Macbeth, Norma is trapped in a grinding ambivalence about her own power which resolves into a helpless, childish, resentful dependency upon some man. And like Helena, the heroine of Shakespeare's *All's Well That Ends Well*, she knows that the man she loves is not a very distinguished specimen. She hints to Joe that she has *purchased* the right to take him for granted, and later she tells Betty by innuendo that Joe is a gigolo.

Yet when Joe threatens to leave her, she cries, "I can't face life without you."

This schizoid status, wherein Norma is both powerful and impotent, manipulator and victim, a knower and a denier of her own knowledge, drives her mad and makes her a destroyer of men, just as Miss Havisham, in her wealthy and powerful impotence, becomes a virulent misanthrope. These fictional "villainesses," unable to discover—or accept—an *autonomous* creative expression of their power, are made monsters by it, to one degree or another.

The question of responsibility for the ambivalence that makes strong women destructive is thorny. C. B. DeMille blames "a dozen press agents working overtime" for Norma's megalomania, as if he were not himself a megalomaniac. He remembers Norma's talent and spirit as "a lovely little girl of seventeen." Her value to the movie industry (unlike his) is almost entirely a function of her youth; consequently she has never grown up and is obsessed with her appearance. But unlike Max, DeMille does not acknowledge any responsibility for Norma's arrested development, her ludicrous existence as a middle-aged child who is still dependent on her director-daddies. Consequently, he will not help her.

DeMille represents both the power of the individual and of the institution. As such, he is the most culpable character in *Sunset Boulevard,* and yet he is the least blamed. Or so it seems. In fact, Wilder assaults DeMille in a series of sly and implicit ways.

Throughout the scene in which Norma visits DeMille's set, we watch DeMille (in jodhpurs and boots) giving orders. His dulcet tones camouflage his control in a grandfatherly benevolence, but everyone around him proceeds in a flurry of humble obedience.

The most telling instance of the nature and scope of this awesome power occurs during a scene with an electrician named Hogeye. DeMille leaves the set momentarily, advising Norma to observe how differently films are currently being made. In his absence, Hogeye recognizes Norma and turns a spotlight on her. Suddenly, members of the cast who formerly worked with her or who remember her films gather around; she is a celebrity once again. But when DeMille returns, he sternly commands Hogeye to "turn that light back where

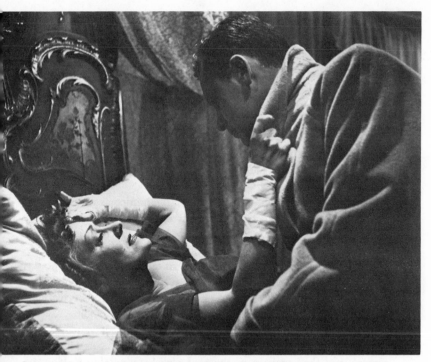

Sunset Boulevard. Norma (Gloria Swanson) slashes her wrists to regain control over Joe, who has attempted to leave her. Her female "weakness" is belied by the grip she has on his coat.

it belongs." Clearly, DeMille decides where the spotlight belongs, and he decides that it does not belong on Norma, although he acts as if he has no power to salvage her career.

DeMille's "helplessness" is further belied in an implicit way by Wilder's casting of Gloria Swanson (as well as Erich von Stroheim and Buster Keaton) in *Sunset Boulevard*. In an act of protest against Hollywood's institutional policy of human discard, Wilder put the spotlight on Swanson, a retired star of silent films, and she became a star once again.

But blaming C. B. DeMille for destroying Norma is as misleading as lionizing Wilder for saving Swanson; it mirrors the distinction between the good plantation master and the bad one—a distinction which ignores the slavery that both masters preserve. The ignored issue in *Sunset Boulevard* is that Hollywood, like every other major American industry, is a patriarchal hierarchy. Women who have worked in Hollywood have always worked for men.

The most a few courageous women—like Bette Davis—could do was fight to keep some control over their own careers. And in television interviews, Ms. Davis speaks ruefully of the enemies she made challenging the industry's male primacy even to the limited extent that she did.

Most women, raised to evaluate their femininity as a function of male approval and love, have been unwilling to flout men, as Bette Davis did, and thus have been trapped in submissiveness, or caught in the middle between assertion and apology. Marilyn Monroe in *The Misfits* (1959) perfectly captures that tentativeness: her dreamy, desperate questions about the way men treat women dissolve into nervous laughter and expiative hugs at the first threat of male hostility.

Norma is also caught midway between challenge and panic. Her neurotic solution is to buy a man, which establishes her power and control, and then make a pretense of girlish vulnerability. Her suicide attempt is emblematic of her ambivalence, since it is both an assertion of power and an act of self-diminution. When Joe returns to her bedside, she seems like a broken doll; but as he acquiesces to her pathos, she clutches him with triumphant talons, revealing to the audience her indomitable strength of will.

It takes an act of madness to free Norma from her neurotic limbo, the very act which forms the basis of *Adam's Rib,* made a year earlier than *Sunset Boulevard.* All the women in *Adam's Rib* are gleeful after a housewife shoots her philandering husband. And while the movie asserts that *no one* has the right to shoot another human being, the symbolic value of this gesture as a liberation from traditional female passivity is simultaneously affirmed.

Neither Marjorie Rosen (*Popcorn Venus,* 1973) nor Molly Haskell (*From Reverence to Rape,* 1974) notes the complex psychopolitical dimensions of Norma's characterization. Both view Norma as a victim of Wilder's satire, "a despairingly lonely serpent" whose predicament is "reduced and trivialized" because the source of her misery is "merely growing old."

It is true that Joe characterizes his relationship with Norma as one between "an older woman who's well-to-do and a younger man who's not doing too well." But to him, the inequality of status is as much at issue as the difference in age. Joe, "the poor dope [who] always wanted a pool," is vulnerable to Norma's enticements because he values the accouterments of her wealth and former success enough to barter his self-respect for them.

The plot of *Sunset Boulevard* can be charted by the stages in Joe's cumulative humiliation. In a Beverly Hills men's store, an obsequious salesman leans close to Joe and urges him to take a more expensive coat "as long as the lady's paying for it." At a bridge party for three of Norma's friends, Joe is expected to stand by like a butler and empty ashtrays. On New Year's Eve, Norma tells Joe that "great stars have great pride" while she strips him of *his* pride before Max and half a dozen musicians. And as Joe tries to leave the house a moment later, the golden watch chain Norma bought for him catches on the door handle, symbolically suggesting the umbilical dependence Joe has on Norma as her kept man and the guilt that makes leaving her impossible. Finally, Joe must hitch a ride into town because his car, "a matter of life and death" to him, has been repossessed by the finance company.

Joe compares Betty to "a brand-new car," an emblem of his masculinity and independence, and his dignity, which in Hollywood is synonymous with and inseparable from success. Betty, by virtue of her youth, represents a number of things which Joe craves and which his humiliating relationship with Norma precludes. But this craving is neither love nor passion. Hence, it is a distortion of *Sunset Boulevard* to see it as a female competition in which youth wins out. In numerous films of the fifties, such as *All About Eve* (1950), *The African Queen* (1951), *The Rose Tattoo* (1955), *All That Heaven Allows* (1956), and *Autumn Leaves* (1956), middle-aged women are shown to be sexually attractive. What renders Norma less than desirable is her neurosis, not her age.

Betty is a *healthier* example of female ambition than Norma is.

Or, to be more accurate, she *would* be a healthier example in a film which took a less negative view of ambition in general. Instead, Wilder uses Betty's ambition to darken her iconic American sweetheart image. Despite her clean-scrubbed face, skirts and blouses, and beribboned hair, Betty is not the girl next door, at least not as we conceived of her in the forties. She tells Joe that she was practically raised on Paramount's back lot: her father was an electrician for the studio, her mother still works in Wardrobe, and her grandmother was a stunt woman for Pearl White. Her family expected her to be a movie star, so she tried, but the studio didn't like her nose. She fixed her nose, but then the studio decided she couldn't act. Now she wants to be a writer. "It's not your career, it's mine [I'm concerned about]," she tells Joe angrily when he refuses to work with her on one of his old screenplay ideas. "I don't want to be a reader all my life. I want to write!" On this same occasion, at Schwab's Drug Store, she tells her boyfriend Artie to "shut up" when he doesn't take her seriously enough.

Like Norma, Betty is driven. Like Norma, her initial attraction to Joe is exploitive; she wants his help to become a writer because "I'm not good enough to do it all by myself." Like Norma, she provides a place for Joe—her office at Paramount where they work together at night. And both women's romances with Joe are equally distasteful, since Norma must purchase his favors and Betty must betray her commitment to Artie.

Artie Green is the "nicest guy" in the film because he lacks the other characters' obsessive ambition. He is satisfied to be an assistant director; perhaps that is why Betty has contempt for him, and why Joe doesn't remember him when he tells Norma that she's the *only* person in Hollywood who has been decent to him.

Norma, Joe, and Betty are drawn together because they are alike. The behavior of each is dictated by the savage, competitive, impersonal world they inhabit, a world in which mutual exploitation is the rule. This spirit of Hollywood is slyly indicted in a subtitle from a fragment of one of Norma's silent films: "Cast out this wicked dream which has seized my heart." A heart seized by a wicked dream—the dream of success—is not free to love, except insofar as

Sunset Boulevard. When Norma's "helpless" act ultimately fails to keep Joe tied to her, she asserts her power over him with a gun. Norma's refusal to victimize herself any longer is a symbolic breakthrough. In one mad moment, she expresses a lifetime of rage at the men who have exploited her.

"love" advances the fulfillment of the dream. Wilder pursues this idea by sabotaging the romance between Betty and Joe.

At Artie's New Year's Eve party, Betty and Joe go off to the *bathroom* to discuss Betty's idea for a screenplay; and in the bathroom they act out a love scene eclectically drawn from a thousand trashy Hollywood costume romances, nearly kissing in earnest before they remember their alliances to other people. By placing this scene in the bathroom and by further parodying romantic love in the exchange of phony platitudes of longing and devotion, Wilder makes a rhetorical comment on the nature of Betty and Joe's attraction to one another. He suggests that Hollywood has injured their capacity to relate to one another in a genuine way. Hence, a certain tackiness and tawdriness adhere to and taint the couple. Even their moonlit walk occurs among the "scenery" of the studio lot.

Hollywood, not Norma, dooms Betty and Joe's romance. It isn't necessary to the story for Joe to reject Betty before Norma shoots him. He could just as well be shot as he was leaving with her. Joe rejects Betty because she represents Hollywood as much as Norma does, and Joe wants to flee Hollywood entirely. But leaving Hollywood is an evasion of the fact that ambition is an inescapable by-product of our competitive economic system. It prevents an honest appraisal of ambition's place in our society, an appraisal which has yet to occur in Hollywood movies.

While millions of women in the past quarter-century have managed to satisfy both their desires for a family and their ambitions for a career, movies like Paddy Chayefsky's *Network* (1976) continue to portray ambitious women as rapacious *film noir* male monsters "in drag." This is because Hollywood remains a male hierarchy whose ambivalence about ambition is unresolved and whose terror of ambitious women is greater than ever. Ironically, Betty and Norma might suffer a far unkinder fate in a Hollywood movie today than they did in 1950, and than they would in real life.

2

The Joys of Marriage

The Quiet Man (1952)

The joys of marriage are the heaven on earth,
Life's paradise . . . the soul's quiet,
Sinews of concord . . .

> John Ford, The Broken Heart (c. 1625)

The film which director John Ford called his "first love story" is in fact a version of *the* first love story: Adam and Eve. *The Quiet Man* is the expression of a longing to return to paradise, heaven on earth, the garden of Eden, which John Ford equated with Ireland, the place of his birth.

But *the gospel according to Ford* has some significant changes from the original. In Ford's version "the fall" occurs prior to the love (and before the film begins). It is *Adam* who has fallen, his sin not disobedience but manslaughter for profit. And Eve is a liberated woman.

The story begins as Sean Thornton (John Wayne), a retired Irish American boxer, returns to live in Innisfree, Ireland, where he was born. He meets and falls in love with Mary Kate Danaher (Maureen O'Hara), a "spinster" who keeps house for her brother Will (Victor

MacLaglen). Sean and Will bid against each other for the purchase of the "wee humble cottage" in which Sean spent his childhood, and because Will has offended the owner of the property, a wealthy widow named Sarah Tillane, by insisting in a pub that she would marry him soon, Sean wins. As a consequence, Will refuses to give Sean permission to wed Mary Kate. Without his permission, she cannot provide a dowry, and she will not marry without one. "I'm no pauper to be going to him in my shift," she insists.

Through a conspiracy instigated by the matchmaker, Michaeleen Oge Flynn (Barry Fitzgerald), Will is persuaded that Sarah Tillane will marry him only if Mary Kate weds first. "What woman would come into a house with another woman in it?" Flynn demands. This deception causes Will to consent to Mary Kate's marriage to Sean. But when Will proposes to the widow after the ceremony, she turns him down, so Will in a rage denies Mary Kate her dowry.

That evening, Mary Kate refuses to consummate her marriage. She feels that, without her dowry, she is not herself but merely a servant. When Sean fails to understand, she slams the bedroom door on him. He breaks down the door and throws her on the bed, but then he leaves her unravished, complaining about her "mercenary little heart." Sean spends his wedding night, and several nights thereafter, in a sleeping bag in the parlor.

Mary Kate wants Sean to fight her brother Will for her dowry. She does not know that Sean will not fight because he killed a man in the boxing ring and has sworn never again to fight "for money." The Protestant vicar Mr. Playfair tries to explain Mary Kate's point of view to Sean, urging him to fight for her love; at the same time, Mary Kate goes to the Catholic priest of the parish, who tells her in no uncertain terms to sleep with her husband. Softened toward one another, the couple finally consummate the marriage. But in the morning, Mary Kate, still believing that Sean is a coward, leaves him. She explains, to Michaeleen the matchmaker that "I love him too much to go on living with a man I'm ashamed of."

Sean finds her leaving Innisfree for Dublin on a train and pulls her off, dragging Mary Kate five miles across the countryside to confront her brother Will. On the way, an old woman gives Sean a stick "to beat the lovely lady."

"Danaher," Sean shouts, "you owe me three hundred and fifty pounds." When Will denies the claim, Sean throws Mary Kate back at him. "It's your custom, not mine," he says. At last the brother relents, handing over the dowry. "There's your dirty money." Mary Kate opens a furnace door, Sean tosses the money in, and Mary Kate slams the door shut.

Mary Kate then leaves what has now become a large crowd of excited spectators and goes "home" to prepare Sean's dinner.

Sean and brother-in-law Will then commence their fisticuffs, but the battle is largely in jest. In the middle of their fight, they stop and have a drink together, arguing about who is going to pay for the refreshment.

In twilight, the husband and brother stagger back to Sean's house drunk. Mary Kate at first greets them angrily, but her anger gives way to amusement. Sean demands his dinner. Mary Kate complies, after sternly telling her brother to wipe his feet.

In the final scene of the film, Will is courting the widow Sarah as Sean and Mary Kate watch fondly. Sean holds the stick which the old woman gave him to beat his wife. Mary Kate takes the stick out of his hands and throws it away. She runs across a brook. Sean pursues her. Together, side by side, they go into their house.

John Ford's *The Quiet Man* is, like many of his films, a marriage of conservative and progressive elements. Ford manipulates antiquated structures (like the antifeminist account of Adam and Eve) into contemporary liberal configurations. In other words, he works toward the future through the past (not unlike psychotherapy).

To begin with, Ford substitutes for Judeo-Christian misogyny the exaltation of the female as mankind's redeemer. This "cult of the goddess," a pagan adoration which reappeared in the secular medieval practice of courtly love, was incorporated by the Church during the Renaissance as the glorification of the Virgin Mary. Mary Kate's name, her conspicuous virginity, and her face—"like a saint"—betray Ford's Christian symbology. And the continual association of Mary Kate with Ireland's landscape and climate establishes her place in pagan nature worship.[1] However, both images are idealistic male fantasies of "a Good Woman" which "imprison woman within a Myth of Woman" (Leslie Fiedler, *Love and Death in the American Novel*, 1960). Ford acknowledges this by having Sean answer his own rhetorical question "Is that real?" with "She can't be," after his first dazzled glimpse of Mary Kate.

Then Ford has Michaeleen the matchmaker introduce the antithetic characterization: Mary Kate as the Irish female stereotype of the hot-tempered red-headed shrew.

The extremes of goddess and shrew cancel out one another and clear the stage for the introduction of a *real* woman who is neither.

When Sean indicates on more than one occasion that Mary Kate's dowry means nothing to him, she interprets his indifference to it as indifference to her as an individual. "Until you have my dowry, you haven't got any bit of me—me, myself," she insists.

Mary Kate equates the dowry with her identity. The piano which she loves to play as she sings and the other furniture she has dreamed of having about her in a home of her own since she was a little girl are extensions of her personality. Without them, and without the money which is a measure of Mary Kate's independence, there is nothing to distinguish her from an anonymous servant:

> I'll wear your ring, and I'll cook, and I'll wash and I'll keep the land. But that is all. Until I have my dowry safe about me, I'm no married woman. I'm the servant I've always been—without anything of my own.

---

[1] When we first see Mary Kate, barefoot, tending sheep, she is a ravishing embodiment of natural beauty in an earthy emerald pastorale. "Hey, is that real?" Sean asks. Sean and Will argue first about land and then Mary Kate. When Sean and Mary Kate first kiss, the wind blows wildly through Sean's house in an external manifestation of Mary Kate's passion. When Mary Kate cries because she can't marry Sean without her brother's consent, it is raining outside as if the sky were crying, too. When she refuses to provide her bonnet for Sean as a courtly token in the Innisfree horse race, the wind blows it off, in an expression of her subconscious longing. When Mary Kate and Sean are courting, he looks hungrily at the landscape before he begins to chase her playfully across a bridge. And when Sean stalks off after Mary Kate insists that he fight Will for her dowry, he takes out his hostility toward her on the countryside, scattering birds and tossing away a lit cigarette.

The Quiet Man. Even though Mary Kate (Maureen O'Hara) refuses to grant Sean (John Wayne) his conjugal "rights," he buys her a horse cart of her own and assumes a passive role as *she* drives *him* to town.

A servant in the broadest sense is someone who functions for the benefit of others and whose "identity" is defined by that function. Ezra Pound, in his poem "Portrait d'une Femme," describes the consequence of such servitude as psychic amorphousness and dismisses the woman about whom he writes in words similar to Mary Kate's: "No! there is nothing! In the whole and all, Nothing that's quite your own. Yet this is you," Pound says.

Mary Kate's battle for status in her marriage—not merely to have but to *be* something of her own—challenges the bases of conventional marriage, just as her behavior in general defies conventional femininity. She "wallops" men, stands up to her bearish brother, shows an aggressive interest in Sean, leads *him* in passion, and leaves him when he fails to respond to her deepest needs. Her break with tradition is epitomized at the end of the film when Mary Kate tosses away the stick which an old woman gave Sean to keep his wife in line. In doing so, Mary Kate rejects the notion of her husband's mastery, to which the older woman has obviously acquiesced. But at the same time she rejects the opportunity to master *him*. Thus, John Ford rescues Mary Kate from the imprisoning myths of both the Good Woman Goddess and the Shrew, to which the film's reactionary symbologies would otherwise relegate her, and thereby creates out of the ashes of the past the image of a *new* woman.

Ford's treatment of sex is an equally sophisticated reversal. For the film encourages conventional expectations and then confounds them. When Sean breaks down the door to the bedroom which Mary Kate has slammed shut against him and throws her on the bed, we expect him to rape her. He would be within his "rights" to do so, and movie tradition would uphold his action. (Rhett Butler rapes Scarlett without censure in *Gone With the Wind* [1939] after she has repeatedly refused to sleep with him.) The audacity of Mary Kate's rebellion is suggested by her request that Sean not "shame" her in front of his friends by telling them of her refusal, and by the Catholic priest's outraged reaction to Mary Kate's confession. Married women traditionally don't have the right to say no. Nonetheless, Sean respects Mary Kate's refusal and, despite his propensity for violence, does not elect to force her.

We expect sexual consummation to occur *after* the issue of the dowry is resolved. But instead it occurs before. In a rare example of adult (as opposed to maternal or paternal) marital compassion, Sean and Mary Kate silently comfort one another although neither understands the reason for the other's resistance, and this *mutual* compassion yields to lovemaking.

Movie convention leads us to expect that Mary Kate will be cheerful and docile the following morning (as Scarlett is), having abandoned the demand for her dowry in favor of sexual satisfaction. But it is Sean who emerges from the bedroom in placid good cheer, only to discover that Mary Kate has left him. Sex alone does not solve the couple's problem. Nor is it held out until the end of the movie as the ultimate *reward* for problem solving (although Ford indicates that *com*passion may yield to passion once problems are eliminated).

This enlightened treatment of sexuality promotes, as few American films have, the superiority of a mature and liberated love relationship by juxtaposing some of our conventional expectations about sex (justifiable rape, sex as a reward and a problem solver) with a few unconventional fulfillments (husbandly forbearance, sex as mutual compassion, and passion as an expression of overall concord).

Concord is the goal of *The Quiet Man*'s narrative journey: [2] a spiritual quietude which Ford equates with the moral innocence and natural harmony of Adam and Eve before the fall. Even the violent, blustering brother Will Danaher achieves a measure of this serenity by the end of the film as we see him courting the widow Sarah. In a twofold image of congruence—Will and Sarah on opposite sides of Michaeleen's prim courtship carriage, and Sean and Mary Kate walking side by side into their house—Ford visualizes the symmetry of successful relationships, a balance which reflects psychic integrity and which renders the equality of the partners inevitable.

Ford depicts the process of achieving integrity in stages of demechanization. Sean arrives on a train, graduates down to a carriage, then a bicycle, a horse, and finally to walking. This movement away from industrialization to domestication suggests that, for Ford, they are in opposition, incompatibles which breed incompatibility.

The pivotal incompatibility of *The Quiet Man's* plot is that Mary Kate's innocent desire to acquire her dowry requires Sean to duplicate the sin which caused his fall: the acquisition of money through violence. Thornton was raised in Pittsburgh on "steel and pig iron hot enough to make a man forget his fear of hell." (Thus does Ford introduce the imagery of industrial America as hell and rural Ireland as the place Sean's mother called "heaven.") Sometime in the past (the historical evasion is purposeful) he used his fists to kill another human being. "I went in there [the boxing ring] to beat

---

[2] In the final moment of the film Catholics "disguised" as Protestants line the road to convince the Reverend Mr. Playfair's superior that he has a large congregation and therefore should not be removed from Innisfree.

his brains out . . . to murder him. For what! The purse, a piece of the gate, lousy money."

Although Ford scrupulously conceals the historical analogue of Sean's profit murder by refusing to locate his story in time, the *movie's* time, 1952, cannot be effaced. *The Quiet Man* was made in the wake of World War II and in the midst of the Korean War and therefore unavoidably reflects certain psychohistorical facts.

The prosperity that attended World War II brought to public attention the possibility that the war had been fought not for ideals but for profit. And in the face of that possibility, America lost its innocence about war in general. John Wayne, the fighting hero of the forties, became Sean Thornton, the rich but guilty retired fighter of the early fifties.

Sean believes that he can escape his guilt in heavenly Innisfree by turning his sword into a plowshare—that is, by becoming a gentleman farmer—and by uniting with an angelic Mary Kate. But he immediately alienates Will Danaher in a territorial dispute (the echo of war) which escalates into a dreaded conflict over money that jeopardizes his love relationship.

The inexorability of consequences attendant upon Sean's crime is symbolized in the courtship sequence when Sean and Mary Kate escape from chaperon Michaeleen's vigilance into a graveyard. As they kiss blissfully in that garden of death—an evocation of the original fall, which introduced death into the world—a thunderstorm suddenly erupts and drenches them, like God's wrath. Awed and chastened, they cling to one another, the passion of their initial embrace subdued.

That happy passion—which in Ford's vision is a corollary of spiritual innocence—is not restored until Sean expiates his offense by incinerating his wife's dowry. His "burnt offering," made literally in behalf of domestic tranquility, frees him from the taint of his past. Only then can he enter into a joyous *egalitarian* union with his wife.

Ford's conception of *male* liberation necessitates the elimination of aggression, greed, and guilt. Such radical alterations are, of course, easy in movies and difficult in real life. How many of us can escape

The Quiet Man. Mary Kate battles with Sean to insure her status as an equal partner in their marriage. Her power is communicated by her strong profile, masculine garb, closed hands, and fighter's stance. She does not resort to feminine wiles to get her way.

to Ireland and burn our *wives'* money to make peace with the gods? But art need not necessarily be prescriptive to set a valuable example. In *The Quiet Man* Ford anticipated the sixties by eschewing war in favor of love and by showing that liberation must be a goal of *both* sexes if they wish to live together in true harmony.

3

Some Pretty Natural Noises
The Marrying Kind *(1952)*

In 1956, at the peak of togetherness, the bored editors of McCall's *ran a little article called "The Mother Who Ran Away." To their amazement, it brought the highest readership of any article they had ever run. "It was our moment of truth," said a former editor. "We suddenly realized that all those women at home with their three and a half children were miserably unhappy."*

Betty Friedan, The Feminine Mystique *(1962)*

The *Marrying Kind*, a film by the makers (George Cukor, Garson Kanin, and Ruth Gordon) of the classic *Adam's Rib* (1949), is a uniquely honest portrayal of American middle-class marriage in the early fifties. Although cloaked in comedy, it is a profoundly sad film, in the way that *Death of a Salesman* is sad, because it is so familiar, and because the characters are so philosophically unequipped to comprehend what has befallen them. For all their crass aspirations, they are remarkably innocent; before life throws them to the lions, they live as if lions didn't exist.

23

85920

This somnambulistic naiveté (personified by Judy Holliday and Marilyn Monroe, each in her own way throughout the fifties) was one of America's most cherished characteristics—a quality which endeared it to itself and which was experiencing its last gasp in the fifties. *The Marrying Kind* bids it a premature farewell, voicing female sentiments almost identical to the following by Marilyn Monroe in *The Misfits* (1959):

> . . . he just wasn't there. You know what I mean? I mean you could touch him, but he wasn't there.

The Marrying Kind also records male responses that anticipate those of the disgruntled widower played by Eli Wallach in *The Misfits:*

> They're all crazy. You try not to believe it because you need them; she's crazy. You struggle, you plan, you build, but it's never enough, it's never a deal; because we gave them the spurs and they're going to use them. I got the marks, I know this racket.

It is as if married couples of the fifties have only one thing to say to each other, which they repeat and repeat, without ever really hearing one another. *The Misfits* and *The Marrying Kind* both begin in the divorce court and end in a tentative recoupling. In each film, a man and a woman struggle to find a means of reconciling their contrary natures and forging a harmonious union. In neither case is the struggle more than fractionally triumphant. Values, priorities, expectations, communication, perception, freedom, ego—marital issues hitherto largely ignored or treated farcically—arise and remain in a state of disturbing irresolution. That irresolution, however, is the open door through which the realities of married life emerged into the spotlight of national awareness.

While comically distorted wedding music chimes in the background, we meet Florence and Chester Keefer (Judy Holliday and Aldo Ray) in the Court of Domestic Relations, where they are seeking a divorce. The judge, a kindly, sensible woman who resents being "the undertaker" for an endless series of dead marriages, asks them to remain after the court has adjourned and explain why their marriage failed. She says there are "three sides to every story, yours, his, and the truth." This tripartite formulation subsequently becomes the basis of the narrative structure of the film. Florence presents her version, Chet his, and we *see* "the truth."

At first we laugh at the harmless discrepancies between the couple's verbal recollections and what we see on the screen of their brief meeting and courtship. Later, we come to understand that subjective and recollective distortion, though normal and inevitable, is a fundamental cause of their breakup.

After the courtship and wedding, we are shown a series of characteristic marital events: the first morning at home after the Keefers' honeymoon, the alarm goes off at dawn so that Chet can get to his job as a postal worker on time. "I gotta get up," Florence insists groggily. "I want to be a good wife." At noon, Florence gives a luncheon for her mother, sister, and sister-in-law. The mother is disdainful of Florence's new apartment, comparing it to her daughter Joan's, who married a wealthy man; and she is contemptuous of Florence's sister-in-law Emily for being married to a butcher. At work, Chet is descended upon by the other "boys" at the post office. They give him ear stopples for peace, "the only way you'll get it now." Later, Chet explains to his best friend George that he's "never had it so good," that he's "got something to go for now . . . like getting someplace, like a family man should." He confides that, "to make it" (i.e., to succeed), a man only has to be smart for ten seconds.

That night, the honeymoon blush begins to fade from the marriage. Chet makes "some pretty natural noises" and Florence tells an interminable story, driving Chet to look for his ear stopples. In his separate twin bed, he asks Florence if she will request a double bed from the landlord and she agrees to ask; but the couple remain in separate beds for the remainder of their marriage, and the separation comes to symbolize their inability to merge into the idealized "one" that the marriage ceremony prescribes.

The movie returns to the courtroom. "Nobody could say there was anything wrong with the way it all started. I mean little things but nothing . . ." Chet concludes. What was the first trouble, the judge asks. Money? Family? "It was just consideration—a question of consideration," Florence responds. "I didn't ever expect him to be interested in only me and nothing else. Maybe it was selfish, but I always thought I ought to come first. And at first I did. But then it got to be ambitions, and making good, and then even other people."

This introduces the next sequence, a going-away-to-Europe party held for Florence's sister Joan and brother-in-law Howard. Chet is asked to stay late at the post office to pick up a spilled container of ball bearings. He keeps Florence waiting on a streetcorner for twenty-five minutes. Nonetheless, they are the first arrivals at the party, but for Florence that isn't the issue. Chet feels uncomfortable with Howard, like a "poor relation," "a fish out of water," although we *see* that Howard is extremely cordial to Chet, and realize this good-natured blusterer is hardly a member of the "high society" Chet envisions him to be. The real problem—never verbalized—is that Chet feels jealous that Howard can take Joan to Europe, and perhaps Florence's resentment toward Chet is a displacement of the same jealousy. Chet subsequently disguises his feelings of inadequacy by becoming very drunk, flirting with a buxom woman, and totally ignoring Florence. Florence *sees* him having a wonderful time (as we do, too), but in fact Chet's feelings are different from his behavior: what we see and what he feels are both "the truth." Here the naive structure which the judge set up earlier begins to crumble into a more complex perception that "versions" *are* truth to the individuals who experience them, and that contradictory versions can be simultaneously "true."

After the party, Chet has an anxiety dream about ball bearings, in which Clarence F. Dow, his wife's ex-boss, is the postmaster general and his brother-in-law Howard is the President of the United States. The "president" falls on the ball bearings Chet, in his haste, failed to retrieve from the post office floor, and Florence becomes his executioner. Waking up from the nightmare, Chet experiences his "ten seconds," an idea for roller skates that use ball bearings.

This dream confirms the inadequacy-anxiety Chet experienced earlier in the presence of his brother-in-law and also the fact that he *feels* pressured by his wife to succeed, as if she were holding a gun on him. This triggers his commercial inspiration, the skates that he counts on to make them millionaires.

But in fulfillment of the "president's" fall in the dream, when Chet and Florence ask Howard to back the invention, Howard nearly kills himself trying them out. In the next scene, an article in *Life* magazine shows that the invention has been marketed by someone else.

"Are you saying," the judge asks, "that what broke things up was just not getting rich all of a sudden?"

"It was more like we were sort of hard luck for each other," Florence replies.

"Let me ask you, Florence, just what did you want out of marriage," the judge inquires.

"What I didn't get," Florence responds. "Well, I always thought if I ever got married the one thing I'd never be any more was lonesome. It's a funny thing, you can be even in the same bedroom with a husband and he seems to be worrying and thinking about different things except you."

"But the different things are always for you," Chet interjects. "The kind of love they got in books and movies, that's not for people. You've got to be more realistic."

Here is the central paradox of the American bourgeois marriage. The wife wants companionship and intimacy. The husband wants to "make good," assuming that the *things* he can then give his wife and family are what matter and what they really want. She wants romance; he wants practical success. She stays at home, bored and lonely, while he works "for her."

In two subsequent scenes, the consequences of this contradiction are explored. Florence is called on the phone by the moderator of a radio quiz show and asked to identify a piece of music. This is *her* "ten seconds" opportunity to strike it rich. She hits upon the right answer, but Chet tells her another. Lacking confidence in her own ability, she blurts out his answer and they lose the money. He is humiliated; she is supportive. "It *could* have been 'Semper Fidelis,' " she says. This scene, which hints at Florence's superiority, is

The Marrying Kind. The spatial triangle of bride–groom–minister is iron-ically duplicated by the triangle of wife–husband–divorce court judge. But beyond the surface irony, the duplication reflects the fact that the

the beginning of a sub-rosa theme in the film: that marriage holds Florence back, forces her to transfer all her aspirations and self-respect onto her husband; and that Chet's fragile ego depends on the un-spoken agreement that Florence will subordinate herself to him. Later, when this agreement is violated, the marriage goes into crisis.

This idea is reinforced briefly in the next scene, when Florence and Chet are preparing to go out to dinner to celebrate their an-niversary. Because the "baby-sitters"—Chet's sister Emily and brother-in-law Pat—are going to be late, Florence says, "I'm treating for a cab." "Since when did you get so manly?" Chet demands.

The remainder of the scene is puzzlingly anticlimactic. Emily and Pat arrive somewhat drunk to celebrate Florence and Chet's "birthday," so the couple stay home. It is a small disappointment, and both Florence and Chet appear to make the best of it and enjoy themselves. Their little boy Joey, awakened by the noises of

couple (Aldo Ray and Judy Holliday) actually do "remarry" as a result of the judge's ministrations.

celebration, emerges from the bedroom and asks why they haven't yet gone out to get married. Everyone laughs and Florence says, in voice-over narration, that things were going all right. "Weren't they?" she asks Chet, for confirmation.

"How should I know?" Chet responds irritably. "Between the job and the home and raising the kids up, the best I was was punchy. I didn't know if things were going good or going bad. They were just going—that's all."

Once again this scene makes the point that feelings and appearances can be different, since we *see* that Chet is enjoying himself but we come to realize that he is not. But the deeper significance of the anniversary scene is that Chet is getting weaker and less resilient while Florence grows stronger. Hence, they experience the disappointment differently. Chet's energy is being drained, without rewards; the family, rather than providing a source of sustenance for him, has become an additional drain and a constant reminder that he is getting older and has not succeeded. Florence, on the other hand, full of unused energy, untried, is beginning to fill the power vacuum that Chet's exhausted depression has created.

This transfer of power is evident in the next sequence, a family picnic on Decoration Day. Florence tells Chet about her scheme for success: flavored postage stamps. Chet replies that only the government would profit from that idea, but Florence resolves to "keep thinking." Then she sings a song called "Dolores," a man's song with the lyric "how I love the kisses of Dolores." It is in the midst of this song that their son Joey drowns.

In the fifties this sequence might have carried a terrifying subliminal message: that when the woman grows independent and begins to feel more like a man, she is punished in this most dreadful of all ways. It is unlikely that the filmmakers intended for the audience to formulate this equation, but it may have reflected a subconscious fear, as popular art so often does.

After recalling for the judge the loss of their son a year earlier, both parents cry. Chet asks, "What's the use?" and Florence says, "I know I got all tired out. He's tired out, too." In fact, Chet fell to pieces after the accident and in a daze was hit by a car. Florence, with her surviving daughter in tow, visited him in the hospital two or three times a day and then took a bus up to Brewster, New York, each weekend for a month while he was convalescing. In this sequence, Florence's constitutional and psychic strength emerge as additional evidence of her superiority. She remains cheerful, goes back to work (although Chet initially protests: "I don't want my wife supporting herself. What am I—some peculiar?"), suffers and transcends the anxiety and guilt of leaving her daughter alone. *Her* exhaustion is reflected in an increasing unwillingness to observe the unwritten law of her marriage: she continues to assert herself and refuses to show absolute deference to her husband.

The breaking point in the marriage occurs when Clarence F. Dow, Florence's former boss, dies and leaves Florence $1,284.63. Chet and his best friend George (still a bachelor) arrive home for dinner. George reveals that Chet is going to receive a promotion.

Florence gives Chet an unopened letter from Dow's lawyer, feeling *he* should open such an important document even though it is addressed to her. She is overjoyed by the contents, but Chet becomes pathologically jealous. Why would Florence's boss leave *her* money, unless something had transpired between them, he demands to know. This sexual suspicion is absurd, but it reflects Chet's feeling of inadequacy as a husband. Once again, Florence has bested him. His promotion pales in the wake of her good fortune. Subsequently, the family falls apart. Chet stalks out, Florence leaves the table in tears, and George the bachelor is left to preside over the dinner table with the Keefers' delightfully obnoxious little girl.

When the Keefers discuss the matter again in the morning, Chet can't decide whether Florence should accept the money or not. Florence reminds him how long it would take them to save that much money, and he replies, "All right! I'm a flop!" That night Chet gives Florence permission to accept the money "for the kid." But when he learns that Florence has gone ahead and taken the money *without* his permission, he becomes furious. "Don't holler," Florence says. "Don't tell me what to do in my house!" Chet counters. "Your house! It's my house, too!" Florence insists. Their daughter wakes up crying and the parents agree not to argue any more; but dissension breaks out again, and this time Florence decides to walk out.

"What kind of mother are you, leaving a kid alone," Chet demands. Totally unaware of the irony that he, as a man, is privileged to walk out on his family whenever he wishes, Chet attacks Florence, playing on maternal guilt.

"What kind of father are you?" Florence responds, hitting him on the same level. But he cannot survive the blow.

"No kind," he replies. "No kind of father, no kind of husband, no kind of man. Nothing."

Florence's final act of assertion, her ultimate assumption of the rights, the power, and the freedom which Chet has surrendered, is to walk out on him and leave him to care for their child. And this she does.

The trouble with this triumph—and it is identical in quality to the one which occurs in *Adam's Rib* (1949)—is that the woman can only win if the man loses. Whether this is the expression of a fear—or a fact—is difficult to know. Is the power structure of relationships a seesaw in which one member at a time must be dominant, or is some balance of power possible? At the end of *Adam's Rib*, Adam (Spencer Tracy) seems to win the power back, at least momentarily, from his wife Amanda (Katharine Hepburn), as a prelude to lovemaking. It is as if the man can't function sexually unless he feels dominant. But at the end of *The Marrying Kind*, the couple appears to achieve a balance. "Maybe if we could have gotten together in the right way and talked everything over," Chet says, when in fact they have done just that. The judge has provided them, twenty years ahead of the fad, with couple counseling, a type of communication therapy that drains the swamp of mutual grievance and provides a broader perspective on the viability of a marriage.

After the judge leaves, the Keefers decide for themselves how they want to resolve things. In a series of stages, Chet and Florence formulate a more realistic marital contract.

Chet tells her that he "can't promise to be no different. The way I am is how I am." "Me, too," Florence responds.

Then Florence says she's "too scared" to get together again. "I mean when we got together finally the first time, I never imagined it could be different, and we could bust up or anything. But now I'd always be thinking about it."

"Maybe it's a good thing to know it's possible," Chet replies.

"Maybe," Florence concedes.

"I'd like to make you a promise that everything's going to be different, I mean, but how can I promise that? I'll tell you what I can do—I can tell you I'd certainly try," Chet says.

"I would, too. From the bottom of my heart."

That is the substance of their remarriage vows, and the beginning of the public re-conception by Americans of marriage in general.

But while the issues of better communication and more realistic expectations are resolved, the problem of Chet's priorities, and the new roles that Chet and Florence will assume in a more balanced marriage partnership, are left open. An important sequence which occurs during the crisis of Clarence F. Dow's legacy is devoted to these problems, although it does not solve them. Chet goes to see Pat, his brother-in-law the butcher, for advice about the money. Pat tells Chet that money means too much to him, that in fact he is obsessed with it. Chet says he wants to "get someplace." Pat replies, "I'm someplace." But Chet cannot comprehend how a man could be satisfied to be a butcher all his life. In response, Pat delivers the following monologue:

> Look, I got a job, one thing, it's steady. Up, down, come or go, one thing people gotta is eat. All right. Quarter after eight in the morning I give Emily a good-bye to the neck and I'm off. Ten minutes to nine, sometimes five, I'm here. Good ventilation, clean working conditions. Twelve o'clock I go have lunch, take a little walk around, look in the windows, come back. Five-thirty we close that door no matter what. Half-hour clean up, ordering, whatever. Six o'clock, hot or cold or Wednesday, I'm out. Ten minutes to seven, sometimes five, I'm home. But see, here's the thing. Once I cross that door going out, I don't care about the shop or the store or the business until I hit it the next day. From the time I leave this store, the only animal I worry about is Emily. I don't want to be a big man. Listen, at twenty hundred and thirty Fifth Avenue, Jackson Heights, I'm the biggest man there is. That's the only place I want to be a big man. So what's wrong with my point of view? All right, so I'm a stick-in-the-mud. No ambition. But for my kind of type, I got married to Emily who's the right kind of type for my kind of type. And she don't push me. She don't tell me what the woman next door got for Christmas. That's it. Live and let live. Is that beautiful or am I prejudiced?

Chet replies, "You don't understand my whole problem, but thanks anyway, Pat."

The *whole problem* which Pat fails to understand is that one of the basic values of American life is the male struggle toward economic success. Unlike Pat, most Americans cannot decide between "a good life" and "*the* good life," although life usually decides for them. That's the fundamental conflict in Arthur Miller's archetypal fifties play, *Death of a Salesman,* and Miller cannot resolve it either. At Willy Loman's burial, one voice says that Willy had the "wrong dreams" and another voice says a man has got to have those dreams —they come "with the territory." American free-enterprise optimism, with its premise that anyone can make it, has never come to terms with the fact that most people don't; that for every Howard Hughes there are a million Willy Lomans and Chester Keefers who experience themselves as failures within the system. And then it becomes the wife's responsibility to pick up the pieces: to protect these men from their own feelings of despondency by feeding their husbands' egos and suppressing and starving their own; to supply the warmth and sustenance and feelings of importance that the society refuses to grant; to make a kingdom of the home because a man must feel like a king *somewhere.* When women stand behind their men in films of the fifties, it is usually to hold them up.

The Marrying Kind asserts, undoubtedly with a degree of truth, that some women, like Pat's wife Emily, are content with their roles as wives within a conventional marriage; but the implication of Pat's monologue is that he gives Emily sufficient attention to make her dependent life worthwhile. Men like Chet, on the other hand, are never home even when they're home. So the ambitious, often superior women they marry end up sacrificing their lives without any of the promised rewards; or at best they are provided with material things in lieu of a husband.

The fact that Florence goes back to work is the beginning of an answer. But it is also the beginning of a whole new realm of difficulties—from the limited job opportunities open to most women and the problem of adequate child care, to the reality of a woman's triple duty as worker, housewife, and mother—that we are now facing in the seventies.

4

The Amiable Spouse

Shane (1953)

I used to admire my head off: before I tiptoed into the wilds and saw the shacks of the Homesteaders. Particularly the Amiable Spouse, poor thing. No wonder she never sang the song of Simple Toil in the Innocent Wilds. Poor haggard drudge, like a ghost wailing in the wilderness, nine times out of ten.

D. H. *Lawrence*, Studies in Classic American Literature *(1923)*

The amiable spouse is another term for the good girl who married dear old dad. In traditional American mythology, "Mom" is the heat-flushed face in the kitchen baking apple pies, the bulwark everlasting of the family, the personification of small town piety, and an asexual monument to happy self-sacrifice. Although a fixture of American film from its inception, "Mom" found her ultimate home in television, beginning with a spate of situation comedies that glorified domesticity in the fifties: *The Adventures of Ozzie and Harriet, Father Knows Best, Leave It to Beaver, The Donna Reed Show,* etc. But even in television, where she played a larger part, "Mom" was a static character. Her importance, as always, was that she was *there*.

35

In George Stevens's *Shane,* the Mom-character, Marian, is a typical emblematic household presence. But while all the *action* occurs between the men, they too are largely abstractions: Good Homesteader Husband, Good Gunfighter, Bad Gunfighter, Bad Cattle Rancher. What complicates *Shane* is a subtext of psychomythic tensions and sociopolitical conflicts, which threaten the stability of the American homestead, causing Marian (and the other major "good" characters) to behave uncharacteristically. As a result, the movie exposes the inadequacy of two American idealistic archetypes— "Mom" and "Dad"—while simultaneously laboring to preserve them.

The film opens with Shane (Alan Ladd) arriving out of nowhere, going nowhere in particular. He is persuaded by Joe Start (Van Heflin) and his wife Marian (Jean Arthur), one of seven families of homesteaders who have established small farms in Wyoming on what a rancher named Ryker considers his own open cattle range, to stay on as a hired hand.

When the homesteaders go into town, Shane trades his gunfighter clothes for a farmer's workshirt and pants. In the saloon he orders soda pop and is taunted by one of Ryker's "boys," Chris Calloway (Ben Johnson), who tosses a whiskey at him so that he'll smell like a man instead of a "sodbuster." But Shane refuses to fight with him.

This prompts one of the homesteaders to aver that Shane is a coward. But the Starts' little boy Joey (Brandon De Wilde) and Marian, who overhear this accusation, reassure Shane that they don't believe it. Afterward, Marian warns Joey not to get to like Shane too much, because he'll be moving on sooner or later and Joey will get hurt.

In the next scene, the settlers go to town again, and Shane for the second time encounters Chris Calloway. But this time he tosses two whiskeys at Calloway and they battle it out. After Shane subdues Chris, Ryker offers Shane double what Start pays him, but Shane turns him down. "What *are* you looking for?" Ryker asks. "Nothing," Shane replies. "Pretty wife Start's got," Ryker muses. "Why, you dirty, stinkin' old man," Shane responds, although Ryker's insinuation is correct. Another battle ensues, involving all of Ryker's men. Joey runs to get his father, and together Joe and

Shane. Joe (Van Heflin) and Shane (Alan Ladd), the passive asexual husband and the aggressive virile gunfighter, compete for the right to Joe's wife (Jean Arthur) and son (Brandon De Wilde). Their struggle reflects conflicting American visions of masculinity (peacetime and wartime) which collided as a result of the paradoxical nature of cold war and the unprecedented sexual demands of married women.

Shane beat Ryker's bunch down. After they leave, Ryker summons a gunfighter named Jack Wilson (Jack Palance) from Cheyenne.

The next morning, Independence Day, Shane teaches Joey how to shoot a gun. Marian, in her wedding dress to celebrate her tenth anniversary, objects. Shane tells her that a gun is no better or worse than the man who wields it, but Marian replies, "We'd all be better off if there wasn't a single gun left in the valley—including yours."

There is a Fourth of July celebration during which Shane dances with Marian. Joe for the first time recognizes the mutual attraction between Shane and his wife.

Tory, a hot-headed southern homesteader, escorts Shipsted, another farmer, into town. There, the gunfighter Wilson baits Tory into drawing his gun. Tory is killed, prompting the other homesteaders to decide to vacate the valley. Joe convinces them all to attend Tory's funeral first, and afterward he and Shane persuade the families to stay on.

Joe feels responsible for the homesteaders' decision and concludes he must stand up to Ryker, even if it means killing him or being killed himself. Marian begs Shane to stop Joe, but Shane says, "I can't tell Joe what's right, Marian."

Joe insists that he won't feel like a man in front of his wife and son if he doesn't go to meet Ryker. He then admits he's aware of Marian's feelings for Shane, and knows she'll be taken care of if anything happens to him.

In the interim, Shane is warned by Chris Calloway that Ryker plans to kill Joe and thus decides he must go to town in Joe's place. But when Shane appears in his buckskins wearing his gun on his hip, Joe fights him for the right to defend the homesteaders. Shane, unable to beat Joe with his fists, eventually hits him in the head with the butt of his gun. Joey is shocked by this treachery and tells Shane that he hates him.

Marian goes toward Shane as if she intends to kiss him, but she is interrupted by Joey. Shane leaves, and Joey, at his mother's urging, goes after him to apologize, following him all the way into town.

"You've lived too long; your kind of days are over," Shane tells Ryker. "My days! What about yours, gunfighter?" Ryker demands. "The difference is I know it," Shane replies quietly. Then he challenges Wilson; they draw their guns, and Shane is victorious. But Joey sees someone hiding above Shane and cries out to warn him. Shane is wounded but he kills the other man and Ryker as well.

Joey, who doesn't realize Shane is leaving the valley for good, tries to convince him to return to the farm. Shane replies:

> I gotta be going on. . . . A man has to be what he is, Joey. He can't break the mold. I tried it; it didn't work for me. . . . Joey, there's no living with a killing. There's no going back. Now, you run on home to your mother and tell her—tell her everything's all right. There aren't any more guns in the valley.

As Shane rides off into the sunset, Joey shouts after him, "Mother wants you (*echo*: wants you, wants you). I know she does. Pa wants you, too. Shane, come back. . . . Bye, Shane."

The movie *Shane* is composed of two different narrative modules: a classic confrontational Western and a domestic comedy. The confrontational Western, which invariably ends with two men shooting it out, is a male myth formula which pits the forces of light and order and "democracy" against the forces of darkness and chaos and tyranny. The domestic comedy consists of family interaction, the solving of interpersonal conflict by the rediscovery of a commonplace moral—for example, "Wives shouldn't be taken for granted" or "Fathers sometimes need to feel like heroes"—but whose actual goal is to affirm the virtues of middle-class family life.

The combining of the two story modules in *Shane* creates a narrative hybrid: Shane, the perennial loner, becomes involved in a domestic upheaval; Joe, a pacifist, attempts to be a heroic gunfighter. As a result, they come into conflict with one another, although they are allies in their opposition to Ryker. Moreover, while Shane kills his adversaries, and Joe maintains his family (thus fulfilling the burdens of their individual myth formulas), they both lose in their struggle with one another (their fistfight makes this clear, since Joe is knocked out, and Shane must hit him with a gun to end the fight). Because they represent two contradictory but equally venerable conceptions of American manhood, neither can be permitted to triumph over the other. Moreover, ascendancy of one over the other is not the goal of the struggle.

Shane and Joe, by "bleeding" into one another's myth modules, are acting out a cultural transition: an attempt to reformulate the characteristics of manhood. *Shane* captures the impact of this transition, not only on men but on a woman and her son. Marian, who ten years earlier married Joe as a matter of course, is now presented with a choice between her husband, the archetypal "good man," and Shane, the archetypal "real man," not merely as mates but as role models for her little boy. Her reaction is to try to choose them both, thereby suggesting the inadequacy of either individual extreme.

The movie corroborates this perception of each man's inadequacy

by making its two most joyous moments when Shane and Joe together remove a tree stump that Joe is unable to remove by himself,
and later when Joe aids Shane against Ryker's boys because Shane is
unable to withstand them alone. There are verbal corroborations as
well, for example, when Marian tells Joe, "You're taking on too
much . . . all by yourself."

On one level of meaning, the necessity for collaboration is an
echo of the alliance between America (Joe) and the Allies (Shane)
against Germany (the *lebensraum*-loving Ryker, who "thinks the
whole world belongs to him"); on another level, the collaboration is
an attempt to integrate the American warrior (Shane) with the
American peacemaker (Joe) in order to cope with the paradox of
the cold war, a permanent instability about which Secretary of State
Dean Acheson warned in 1946:

> We have got to understand that all our lives the danger, the
> uncertainty, the need for alertness, for effort, for discipline will
> be upon us. This is new for us. It will be hard for us.[1]

But on a much more primary level, the merger of Shane and Joe is
the marriage of power and idealism, of sex and love.

Our American mythology, which is dominated by the polarities
characteristic of romance, has consistently depicted idealism as impotent and the idealist as asexual (or female). Two classic examples
are Ashley Wilkes in *Gone With the Wind* (1939) and Victor
Laszlo in *Casablanca* (1943), both shown in contrast to virile, violent,
cynical men—Rhett Butler and Rick Blaine. Joe and Shane present
a similar dichotomy, with Joe introduced to the audience "defending"
his home with a small unloaded shotgun that belongs to his eight-
year-old son. Even in a film like Frank Capra's *Mr. Smith Goes to
Washington* (1939), in which there is only one hero, the idealist
Jefferson Smith is portrayed as a prepubescent boy scout, a virgin,
while all the real power belongs to a corrupt, sophisticated newspaper
magnate who proves to be invincible.

---

[1] Eric F. Goldman, *The Crucial Decade—and After* (New York: Vintage,
1960).

Complex women like Scarlett in *Gone With the Wind* and Ilsa in *Casablanca* are characteristically—and understandably—torn between the two sorts of men, their maternal, domestic natures attracted to the vulnerable, gentle idealists; their self-centered sexual and independent instincts aroused by the virile cynics. Thus, the "good" and "real man" distinction spawns the "good" (maternal) and "real woman" (sexual) distinction, either dividing women against themselves or splitting them into mutually exclusive extremes, like the "Mom" and the "Tramp."

Marian (like Shane and Joe) is an extreme in transition: she is in the process of recovering her lost sexuality and independence. Pleading with Shane and Joe as they struggle with each other for the right to defend the household against Ryker and Wilson, she says:

> You're both out of your senses. This isn't worth a life—anybody's life. What are you fighting for—this shack, this little piece of ground, and nothing but work, work, work. I'm sick of it . . .

If the farm isn't worth *anybody's* life, it isn't worth Marian's either. Tired of her marriage and of married life itself, she begs Joe, "Let's go—let's move on." But Joe has already stated that he will not leave the farm except in a "pine box." Only Shane can take her somewhere else, for Shane, unlike Joe, wants to go "someplace [he has] never been."

Joe is unwilling to accept the change in his wife: "Marian, don't say that. That ain't the truth. You love this place more'n me."

"Not any more!" Marian replies emotionally.

Marian's disenchantment with marriage, while uncharacteristic of her type in films prior to the fifties (and in television situation comedies throughout the fifties and sixties), is not unique. There is evidence of "good women's" sexual distress and domestic rebellion in other fifties films: *From Here to Eternity, Rebel Without a Cause,* and *All That Heaven Allows,* for example. Moreover, this disturbance in the archetype is part of a larger disturbance of archetypes. In the film *Bigger Than Life* (1955), an Ozzie and Harriet family is turned into a black comic nightmare by the necessity for the good-natured husband to take cortisone, a drug which causes him to express his repressed sexuality and anger, reject his prim wife, try to murder his son, and disparage the narrowness of his middle-class life. In another archetypal shift, Gloria Grahame, a tramp in *The Big Heat* (1952), and Donna Reed, a prostitute in *From Here to Eternity,* attempt to transform themselves into "good women" with some success. Significantly, they do not repent; they simply reveal themselves to be both good *and* sexual. The mere fact of casting Donna Reed, an All-American-Girl, as a whore indicates a changing perception of the "fast" woman, which Marilyn Monroe epitomizes. As Norman Mailer writes in *Marilyn* (1973):

> She might be as modest in her voice and as soft in her flesh as the girl next door. . . . Even down in the Eisenhower shank of the early Fifties she was already promising that a time was coming when sex would be easy and sweet. . . . she was the angel of sex. . . .

A girl-next-door angel of sex is an amalgamation of the "virgin" and the "tramp."

Marian in *Shane* is the beginning of another amalgamation: the "amiable spouse" and the "lover." And as a neophyte "'new woman," Marian requires a new man, one with a sexual dimension which her husband lacks. Marian's immediate attraction to Shane, exemplified by her dinner invitation to this perfect stranger, the special pains she takes with the dinner—which Joe notes with surprise ("Say, we're kind of fancy, ain't we? Good plates, an extra fork . . ."), her suggestion that Joe hire Shane to help out on the farm, and her appearance the following day in a dress (before this she wears pants), is made explicitly sexual following a scene between Marian and Joey. The little boy tells Marian, "I love Shane. I love him almost as much as I love Pa." Marian agrees: "He's a fine man. . . . Yes, I like him, too." Immediately afterward, she appears to be on her way out to the barn, where Shane sleeps, when Joe intercepts her. "Joe—hold me," she says passionately. "Don't say anything. Just hold me—tight."

It is not merely Joey's admission of love for Shane that prompts Marian's eruption of desire, but the curious fact that Joey—with his straight blond hair and blue eyes—looks very much like Shane (and almost nothing like his curly-haired brunet, brown-eyed father). Buried in this resemblance is a sexual element which Philip Slater illuminates in *The Glory of Hera* (1968) in his chapter on the Greek mother-son relationship: the married woman who lacks a satisfying emotional and sexual alliance with her husband often seeks it with her son. Joey is a little Shane, Marian's confidant, her little man, and the vehicle through whom Marian expresses her sexual longing ("Mother wants you!") for his mature counterpart. Joey, in turn, wants to learn to shoot a gun like Shane, wants implicitly to be a man like Shane, a man a woman *wants*. His mother's objection to Joey's initiation to gunfighting (which occurs on Independence Day) may therefore be, at least in part, a resistance to his sexual maturation, just as her objection to Shane's gun is, to some extent, a resistance to sexual temptation. Incest and adultery are forbidden alternatives. But eventually Marian sends Joey after Shane. As Philip Slater writes, ". . . though *she* might be confined and restricted, her son, an extension of herself, was free and mobile, and she could live her life through him."

In other words, Joey is transformed from a crypto-sexual object to a mode of vicarious independence, once Marian's desire for sex and independence becomes overt. The disturbing revelation is that Joey is "used" by his mother as a substitute for the elements her own life lacks. The son cannot be a free agent so long as the mother is not free.

Moreover, Joey is caught in a cross fire of mixed messages. Marian says, "Don't be like Shane" and then sends Joey after him. Shane teaches Joey to shoot a gun and then tells him, "Don't be like me—go home to your parents." This schizophrenic ambivalence derives from America's attitude toward violence.

Our culture, although obsessed with violence, has been unable to integrate violence into its idealistic structures. The virtue of the gunfighter, therefore, is that he is essentially a deus ex machina, an independent hero whose talent for killing makes him temporarily

useful to the otherwise unprotected idealistic institutions, but who can be counted on to ride off into the sunset with a hearty "Heigh-ho, Silver!" as soon as his services are no longer needed. As with ambition and sex, the popular American fantasy of violence allows for no middle ground, no possibility of moderation or control. Therefore, "good man" Dave Bannion in *The Big Heat*, although reduced to vigilante action after the death of his wife because his police superiors have been corrupted by the wife's murderer, cannot in 1952, any more than Joe Start in 1953, be *permitted* to do his own killing. Moreover, the woman who kills *for* Bannion is in turn killed. As Shane tells Joey, "There's no living with a killing." Or a killer.

Shane. Shane and Joe, two halves of a whole man, joyously join forces to remove a tree stump that neither can uproot separately. Their collaboration is the expression of a longing for the reconciliation of their divergent male images.

Shane. Shane usurps Joe's father role by teaching Joey how to shoot a gun. Joey is torn between his love for his father and his attraction to Shane as a role model, just as his mother is torn between her loyalty to her husband and her sexual desire for Shane.

In the seventies, however, along with the sexual revolution, there has been a revolution in the portrayal of violence. "Good men" have become killers, savaged by the corruption and brutality of the society in which they live. There is a positive aspect to the *symbolic* investment of idealists with virility and power; but in keeping with the popular fantasy of violence as ungovernable, the inevitable outcome in these new films, from *Straw Dogs* (1971) and *Walking Tall* (1973) to *Death Wish* (1974) and *Jaws* (1975), has been a bloodbath in which the "family man" outkills the killers.

The potential—and the longing—for this transition in the "good man" is inherent in *Shane,* most obviously when Joe tries to become a gunfighter. But it is apparent in other details of the film as well. Ryker's gang expresses contempt for the "sodbusters," suggesting they hide behind their womenfolk and are implicitly "womanish"—or cowardly. Nor does the film vindicate the homesteaders of this charge: with the exception of Tory, they are portrayed as a chicken-hearted bunch. They are, however, as contemptuous of cowardice as the ranchers, as is evident when they accuse Shane of it after he refuses to fight with Chris Calloway. In fact, they project their self-contempt onto Shane, which drives him to engage in a battle with Calloway and the rest of Ryker's band at their next encounter. Joe comes under the same pressure, despite Tory's example of the wages of foolish bravery. On his anniversary, Joe proclaims that he would not trade places with any man on earth, but eventually he tries to become Shane:

> Marian—honey—it's *because* you mean so much to me that I've got to go [kill Ryker]. You think I could go on living with you, and you thinking I'd showed yellow? Then what about Joey? How do you think I'd ever explain that to him?

The "male identification" of Joe with Shane is what Philip Slater calls "the homosexual search" ("Pa wants you, too"), "a search for a more heroic self-image." But Joe misunderstands Marian's need: she does not want a gunfighter; she wants a *lover*. The symbolic conflation of gun and phallus, the double meanings of the words potence and impotence—that is, our psychic equation of sex and violence—make the misunderstanding inevitable and any attempt to separate the two hellish.

Nonetheless, the hope at the end of *Shane* is that Joey may find some middle ground between violent romance and domestic inadequacy; for he is left *literally* in the middle between Shane and his father. A decade later in *Hud* (1963), a teenage Brandon De Wilde is still struggling with the same polarities and is once again left in the middle between his idealistic, ascetic grandfather and his hedonistic, cynical uncle, with the hope that he will discover a realistic compromise.

The hope is fulfilled, not surprisingly, in a "woman's film," *Alice Doesn't Live Here Anymore* (1974). Despite its disappointingly conventional ending, in *Alice* a "good woman," widowed with a son, strikes out to establish a singing career and on the way finds a "good man" who is also endowed with authority and sexual charisma: the longed-for amalgamation of Joe and Shane. Moreover, it is possible in this movie for Alice to be both a mother and a lover, a "good woman" and a "real woman."

The characters in *Shane* were on the brink of these possibilities, but without cultural awareness or support. And so the makers of the film retreated to a reactionary consolation: "A man has to be what he is, Joey. He can't break the mold."

5

The Hard and the Soft

From Here to Eternity *(1953)*

When a nation shows a civilized horror of war, it receives directly the punishment of its mistake. God changes its sex, despoils it of its common mark of virility, changes it into a feminine nation, and sends conquerors to ravish it of its honor.

Juan Donoso-Cortés, Masculine/Feminine: Readings in
Sexual Mythology and the Liberation of Women *(1969)*

The most memorable moment in Fred Zinnemann's Academy Award winning film *From Here to Eternity,* and indeed one of the most famous moments in the history of American film,[1] is the scene in which a bare-chested Burt Lancaster in a series of perfectly choreographed stages drops onto his knees and then onto the lips of a damp Deborah Kerr on the sands of a moon-drenched, deserted Hawaiian beach. This perfect, and virtually unprecedented, depiction of romantic *sexual* passion does not exist in James Jones's Na-

---

[1] The beach scene in *From Here to Eternity* has been alluded to, reproduced, and parodied in everything from Sid Caesar and Imogene Coca's *Show of Shows,* Robert Aldrich's *Autumn Leaves,* and Billy Wilder's *The Seven Year Itch* in the fifties to *The Carol Burnett Show, Happy Days,* and *The Academy Awards Show* in the seventies.

tional Book Award winning novel [2] from which the film was adapted, although the novel was notorious for its shockingly explicit depictions of sex. Sexual passion in Jones's novel is invariably bait for the emotional and economic trap of marriage and is, therefore, never portrayed romantically. In contrast, Zinnemann's treatment of this film scene is so powerfully seductive that its romantic radiance obscures a multitude of social and psychic dilemmas.

In fairness to Zinnemann and his film, one must point out that this beach scene deteriorates into a vitriolic exchange, during which the male character accuses the female one of being a tramp and the female charges the male with brutal insensitivity. In its movement, then, the scene casts a shadow upon the very ideal it appears to create. People, however, have remembered the ideal.[3]

But in fairness to the audience, one must acknowledge that it is *easy* to misunderstand this film. Or rather, it is easy to come to no clear understanding of the film and, as a consequence, be tempted to impose the most sentimental, least disturbing meaning upon it. For the film adaptation distorts, ignores, and eliminates crucial material from the novel.

I have elected, therefore, to use the novel to clarify the film. Taken together, these two landmark documents of the fifties suggest a tumultuous dissatisfaction on the part of both men and women with a society which indiscriminately channels their passionate energy into middle-class marriages—marriages which shackle couples to an economic grindstone that annihilates individual identity and love. Moreover, when the novel and film are considered together, it becomes apparent why the film—a product of a mass culture medium charged with maintaining public morale [4]—obfuscated its social

---

[2] The beach excursion in Jones's novel is not dramatized but merely described in retrospect as a comic disaster, in which damp sand and chill conquer passion.

[3] A particularly comic illustration occurs in a television commercial advertising a Connecticut jeweler. In it, a diamond ring is placed next to a paperback copy of Jones's novel, to signify an eternity of marital love.

[4] "Nobody seriously questions the principle that it is the function of mass culture to maintain public morale, and certainly nobody in the mass audience objects to having his morale maintained." Robert Warshow, *The Immediate Experience* (New York: Atheneum, 1970).

critique. For *From Here to Eternity* arises out of the transitional discontent which eventually fueled both the political and feminist revolutions of the sixties.

The film also helps clarify the *novel* in one very important way. In its omission of most of the novel's social critique, it unwittingly uncovers a primary source of social malaise: a polarized concept of masculinity (all that is hard) so divorced from human reality (a mixture of hard and soft) that it is threatened by interaction with anything but itself; and an association of everything which falls outside that concept (including many aspects of civilization itself) with the female, who represents the ultimate threat to masculinity.

The story traces the destinies of its four major characters: Milt Warden (Burt Lancaster) and Karen Holmes (Deborah Kerr), Robert E. Lee Prewitt (Montgomery Clift) and Alma "Lorene" Burke (Donna Reed), four Americans in Hawaii in 1941. In the film version, Prewitt, a buck private in the U.S. Army, transfers into a new company, where Milt Warden is sergeant. Prewitt's new company commander, Dana Holmes, is an executive prototype obsessed with team spirit ("In the Army it's not the individual who counts"). He wants Prewitt to box for his outfit. But Prewitt, a champion of individualism ("A man don't go his own way, he's nothing"), refuses because he blinded a man in the ring a year earlier. As a result of his principled obstinacy, Prewitt is given "the treatment"—a series of undesirable tasks laced with continual emotional harassment and physical abuse.

Prewitt's friend Maggio (Frank Sinatra) introduces him to a "social club" (a whorehouse in the novel) run by a pretentious woman named Mrs. Kipfer. There he meets Alma, who is called "Lorene"— a name derived from a perfume ad. At the same time, Milt Warden begins a love affair with Captain Holmes's wife, Karen, who is reputed to be a tramp. Both men fall in love.

Alma, however, will not marry Prewitt because he is a common soldier. She was jilted by a wealthy boy back in America and wants to make enough money in Hawaii to return home "in style" and make a "proper" marriage "because when you're proper, you're safe."

Karen and Milt also encounter a marital impasse. According to the story, Milt as a "noncom" risks twenty years in Leavenworth for sleeping with a commissioned officer's wife. But apparently he is safe from that consequence if he, too, becomes a commissioned officer. Hence, Karen urges him to alter his status so that she can divorce her husband and marry him. Milt, however, despises the idea of being an officer.

Both Prewitt and Warden feel pressured by the women they love to compromise their integrity and seek career advancement. Since both men love the Army as a kind of masculine American ideal which power (exemplified by Dana Holmes) has corrupted, neither wants to advance to a position of power. Nonetheless, both men, after commiserating drunkenly about the pain of love, agree to acquiesce. But fate intervenes. Prewitt's friend Maggio dies as a result of injuries inflicted by an Army bully named "Fatso" (Ernest Borgnine, depicting another example of corrupt power, since "Fatso" runs the Stockade). In revenge, Prewitt stabs "Fatso" to death, goes AWOL, and hides out in Alma's apartment.

Karen's husband is subsequently booted out of the Army for mistreating his men (in the novel, he is promoted) and makes arrangements to return to America. Karen meets with Milt to find out if she should get a divorce. A confusing scene ensues. Milt admits he has not signed the papers preliminary to becoming an officer (although it is no longer necessary for him to do so, with Holmes out of the picture). Karen tells him, "You're already married—to the Army." Warden objects weakly: "I love you—I don't want you to go back to Holmes." Karen responds that with all the hiding and stealing around it would never work out (although clandestine behavior is no longer required). Milt lets Karen tearfully talk herself out of the relationship, and they part.

The Japanese attack Pearl Harbor. Prewitt in a burst of patriotism decides to return to his company. Alma begs him to stay and offers to marry him *as he is,* but he ignores her entreaty and leaves.

In the darkness, he is mistaken for a Japanese ground invader (the American Army erroneously believed Hawaii would be invaded by land after the bombing) and is killed by his own men. In a

eulogy over Prewitt's dead body, Warden praises his stubborn in-
dividuality and curses him for his inability to "play it smart" (presumably, Prewitt's inability to be sneaky about his insubordination,
as Milt has been).

In the final scene of the film, Karen and Alma bid Hawaii a
forlorn farewell from the deck of a boat destined for the mainland.
Orchestrated by syrupy Hawaiian music, Alma, in a series of lies,
transforms her unfruitful affair with an Army-loving "dogface" into a
tragic romance with a Pearl Harbor hero. In doing so, she reveals her
total misunderstanding of the peculiar nature of Prewitt's heroism
(pitting stubborn individualism against the pressures of corruption),
and the significance of his death, both as an indictment of America
(which destroys its own heroes) and as the *ultimate evasion of her.*

Alma's misunderstanding, while intended to be ironic, turns out to
be prophetic. Like Zinnemann's deflation of the beach scene, this
undercutting of romantic distortion is too subtle, so what remains is
the distortion itself: true love thwarted by the vicissitudes of conventional heroism.

Again and again, the timid subtlety of the film's social critique is
overwhelmed by the possibility of banal and romantic interpretations.
The movie's treatment of marriage is an illustration. While Alma
tells Prewitt at one point that living together is better than being
married, how can one believe her when she is obsessed with the
accumulation of enough money to raise her social status so that she
may marry well? Karen is similarly obsessed. She tells Milt bitterly
about her intolerable marriage to Dana Holmes, a union marred by
every marital nightmare from mutual contempt to multiple adultery.
Yet she longs to escape from one marriage only to enter into another.
From the perspective of the seventies, one can deduce that these
women are obsessed with marriage because they have no alternative
vision of life; in other words, they are trapped. But no one could
have been *expected* to deduce this in the marriage-obsessed fifties.
That is why James Jones in his novel spelled it out.

Karen, at the beginning of the novel, imagines leaving her husband
in terms which make it clear that her sexual role has trapped her:

> In her imagination she saw herself rising up, telling him [her husband] what she thought of him, packing a bag and leaving, to live her own life and earn her own way. She would get a job and an apartment someplace. What kind of job? she asked herself. In your physical condition what can you do? What training have you? Besides to be a wife?

She blames her hysterectomy, an operation she was forced to undergo when her husband gave her gonorrhea, for her feelings of unhappiness:

> Furtively, as if it had an intelligence of its own, her hand moved up her stomach and touched the ridge of scar tissue. . . . The grape torn open and the seed plucked out, withering before it ever came to fruition.

But then she acknowledges that she has a child, a son, and that her despair must therefore have another source:

> That isn't so, she told herself, you know it isn't so. You've borne his heir for him, who can say your life is fruitless? How can you be fruitless? You've been a mother, haven't you?
>
> There must be more, there must be, something told her, someplace, somewhere, there must be another reason, above, beyond, somewhere another Equation besides this virgin + marriage + motherhood + grandmotherhood = honor, justification, death. There must be another language, forgotten unheard unspoken, than the owning of an American's Homey Kitchen complete with dinette, breakfast nook, and fluorescent lighting.
>
> Among the broken bathroom fixtures and the sticky brightly colored rainwashed labels on the emptied cans, Karen Holmes was looking through the city dump of civilization, desperately hunting for her life.

Because Karen feels herself incapable of being anything but a "wife," the only means she has of making more of her life is through the love of a man other than her husband:

> At least there was one way left for a woman to express herself, she thought distastefully, now that the chastity belts were outlawed, now that the stocks and ducking chairs were gone, although the condemnation was still as bad.

But when Karen's affair with Milt Warden ends, she is left in essentially the same place where she began: without a life.

The film, on the other hand, never indicates the economic and emotional traps which prevent Karen from leaving her husband, or which limit her life options to one man or another. In addition, Karen's child is deleted from the adaptation, which distorts the nature of her unhappiness. "I'll tell you about waste, Sergeant," Karen says to Milt in the movie, ". . . what about the house without a child?" By making Karen childless, the film can have Karen long for motherhood, rather than an independent life, as in the novel. This shift away from *existential* discontent is made because Karen's feelings in the novel invoke the revolutionary possibility that marriage and motherhood are not enough to fill a woman's life. What the film substitutes is exactly the opposite conviction: that marriage and motherhood are all a woman needs and that female unhappiness such as Karen's can only derive from the absence of one or the other.

The other side of the coin of marital entrapment which the film eliminates is its effect on men and their feelings about women. The Prewitt of the movie—played with vulnerability and sweetness by Monty Clift—appears to have a perfectly straightforward relationship with women. He meets a girl, he falls in love with her, and he proposes marriage. Even the kinky aspect of falling in love with a whore is mitigated, since Alma is supposed to do nothing more than participate in "gentlemanly relaxation with the opposite gender." But in the novel, Prewitt's hostility toward women and marriage is a vital part of his psychological makeup and of Jones's social critique. Early in the text, Prewitt explodes at a Hawaiian girl with whom he is "shacked up":

> Why in the hell would I marry you? . . . Have a raft of snot-nosed nigger brats? Be a goddam squawman and work in the goddam pineapple field the rest of my life? Or drive a Schofield taxi? Why the hell do you think I got in the Army? Because I didn't want to sweat my heart and pride out in a goddam coalmine all my life . . . like my father, and his father, and all the rest of them. What the hell do you dames want? to

From Here to Eternity. The famous beach scene which most audiences recall as a depiction of perfect sexual passion is followed by alienation, resulting from the ambivalence of the man (Burt Lancaster) toward a sexual woman (Deborah Kerr). This is the first in a series of irreconcilable conflicts which ultimately drive the couple apart.

take the heart out of a man and tie it up in barbed wire and give it to your mother for Mother's Day?

This same resentment of women's maternal, domestic, civilizing "instinct" poisons Prewitt's feelings for Alma later in the novel (where in the film it is only Pearl Harbor that intervenes). For Prewitt perceives women as *biologically* motivated culprits in an assault on masculine independence.

Milt Warden, who shares Prewitt's anger toward women in the

novel, puts it in a different perspective in a conversation with Karen by describing women as pawns of American capitalism:

> I've stood up against all of that, I've stood up for me Milt Warden as a man, and I've made a place for myself, where I can be myself, without brownnosing any man, and I've made them like it.
>
> And now I'm supposed to go on and become an Officer, the symbol of every goddam thing I've always stood up against, and not feel anything about it. I'm supposed to do that for you.
>
> You're the bait in the trap . . .

The concept of a *society* which conditions women to seduce men into an upwardly mobile economic spiral, a society which manipulates men and women into a self-annihilating intimacy for the sake of its own perpetuation, has no place in the film. In Zinnemann's movie, American society, the capitalist economy, and various social institutions—such as marriage, motherhood, and the Army—are taken off the hook. There may be a bad marriage, or a corrupt officer or two, but the basic structures are sound. Moreover, there is no cause, social or emotional, for the failure of the story's two love affairs; the relationships fail due to *extenuating circumstances!*

On the other hand, the novel's indictment of society is a denial at a deeper level, insofar as it absolves men of responsibility for the shape of that society. In addition, the novel's attempt to displace blame from women onto society merely camouflages an abiding sense of alienation from women which Jones is unable to resolve.[5] For example, Warden's depiction of women as pawns of American capitalism, while intended to exonerate women of primary responsibility for their actions, actually allies them with corrupt powermongers like Holmes, in that both collaborate to destroy masculine integrity. And that alliance has its origins in the story of the fall of man, wherein innocent Adam is assaulted by the combined forces of Eve ("the bait in the trap") and the Devil.

---

[5] ". . . even men who consciously have a very positive relationship with women and hold them in high esteem as human beings, harbor deep within themselves a secret distrust of them . . ." (Karen Horney, *Feminine Psychology,* New York: Norton, 1967).

That seemingly ineradicable perception of women as the Enemy is a mainstay of Jones's plot, and thus there was no way to *avoid* adapting it into the film: *From Here to Eternity* concerns two men's desire for women who are ostensibly unattainable; when the women *do* become available, the men turn away from them. Moreover, there is no attempt to deny that these men love the Army more than they love women. And lest one believe the characters' preferences differ from the author's, it is instructive to note that Jones dedicated his novel "To the United States Army."

It is a commonplace of literary criticism that men in American novels fear women and prefer the company of other men. As Leslie Fiedler writes in *Love and Death in the American Novel* (1960):

> The figure of Rip Van Winkle presides over the birth of the American imagination; and it is fitting that our first successful homegrown legend should memorialize, however playfully, the flight of the dreamer from the shrew—into the mountains and out of time, away from the drab duties of home and town toward the good companions and the magic keg of beer. Ever since, the typical male protagonist of our fiction has been a man on the run, harried into the forest and out to sea, down the river or into combat—anywhere to avoid "civilization," which is to say the confrontation of a man and woman which leads to the fall to sex, marriage, and responsibility.

Fiedler's observation about American novels is extended to American films by Michael Wood in his book *America in the Movies* (1975):

> It is women who assert the myth of community in the movies, who propose a world of children and homes and porches and kitchens and neighbors and gossip and schools—everything the American hero is on the run from; and it is men in groups who represent a temporary, wishful exemption from this grim destiny.

Only from this perspective is it possible to understand why Milt Warden and Robert E. Lee Prewitt love the Army. Alma certainly doesn't understand: "What do you want to go back to the Army for?" she asks Prewitt in the film after the Pearl Harbor bombing. "What did the Army ever do for you besides treat you like dirt and give you one awful going over, and get your friend killed? What do you want to go back to the Army for?" American women never *do* understand because they have been conditioned to ignore men's ambivalence toward them and its consequence—that no matter what they do, they cannot really win:

> Man must work, and woman must exploit his labour. . . . And if woman submits, she can be cursed for her exploitation; and if she rebels, she can be cursed for competing with the male; whatever she does will be wrong. . . .[6]

How could Karen and Alma possibly understand that their *un*-availability and *in*dependence are what make them so attractive to Milt and Prewitt, that these men "only love the things we cannot have," as Milt tells Karen in the novel? How could Alma know that when Prewitt says, "A man loves a thing; that don't mean it's got to love him back," he is really saying that the last thing he wants is *requited* love; and that the Army, which he loves and which does not love him back, is a sort of romantic ideal?

Marriage stands in opposition to romance, because marriage is real and romance is based on fantasy. On the other hand, romantic love is the basis of American marriage, which means that a majority of marriages begin in fantasy and must somehow survive the long drop down from the clouds. Milt Warden in the novel rails against "the epidemic of romantic love [that] is threatening to decimate the United States" but what he ultimately rejects by breaking with Karen is not romantic love but marriage, which "lost you all your illusions."

In the novel we are permitted to see the loss of illusions that occurs for all *four* characters when they spend extended periods of time together, thus approximating "the situation that would exist when the honeymoons were all over, just like husband and wife." Karen discovers that her problems are not resolved by a new "marriage" and begins to drink heavily. Milt decides he does "not want a wife who was going to turn into an alcoholic anonymous." Prewitt grows bored with the uneventful soft life at Alma's apartment and

---

6 Dorothy Sayers, *Unpopular Opinions* (New York: Harcourt, Brace, 1947).

becomes homesick for Army maneuvers: "He bet they were having a rough time out at Makapuu, building pillboxes in that rock. But the roughness, strangely, instead of making him glad he was out of it, excited him and made him want to get in on it." Alma complains to Prewitt that he has totally withdrawn from her: "I hardly talk to you from one day to another. You look at me as though you were half asleep—like now. As if you hardly knew who I was."

This parallel discovery—that a love affair is different from a marriage and that marriage does not necessarily fulfill one's romantic fantasies, may not even satisfy one's basic human needs—is condensed by the film to a brief dialogue between Karen and Milt about misery. "I wish I didn't love you," Milt says. "Maybe I could enjoy life again." Karen replies, "So they were married and lived unhappily ever after." But the dialogue ends in *affirmation*. "I wouldn't trade a minute of it," Milt concludes. "Neither would I," Karen agrees.

That affirmation, followed by Karen and Milt's ambiguous breakup which tries to make parting seem like a circumstantial inevitability, and Prewitt's *apparently* heroic renunciation of Alma for the Army after the bombing of Pearl Harbor, serve to obscure the message of the novel that the last thing in the world the marriage-obsessed fifties wanted was middle-class marriage, with its "world of children and homes and porches and kitchens and neighbors and gossip and schools . . ." (Michael Wood, *America in the Movies*). Instead, the movie audience is vicariously permitted to evade marriage without becoming aware that this is what it is doing.

For men, the end of the film is a perfect fantasy retreat to the good old days of World War II, a celebration of the event which provided them with an honorable escape from domestic life. Milt Warden's face glows as he rallies the soldiers in his company after the Japanese surprise attack. He exudes pride, strength, mastery, and indomitable charisma. For he is back in the saddle again, where men are men and the women have all been evacuated.

The end of the movie is also a fantasy of retreat for women, back to wartime when they were free to memorialize their failed affairs of the past as ideal romances, and to fantasize the fulfillment of their romantic ideals in the future, without the disillusioning presence of men to douse their fantasies in reality.

But reality intervenes nónetheless, at the very last instant, when Karen (who knows about Prewitt through Milt) suddenly realizes that Alma is lying:

> My fiancé was killed on December 7th. . . . He was a bomber pilot. He tried to taxi his plane to the edge of the apron. The Japs made a direct hit on him. Maybe you read about it in the papers. He was awarded the Silver Star. They sent it to his mother. She wanted me to have it. . . . They're very fine people. Southern people. He was named after a general. Robert E. Lee—Prewitt.

In Karen's shock of recognition resides the potential for recognition of all the lies women have told, and believed, in the name of romantic love.

The final image of the film captures the spirit of female transition in the fifties in the most literal sense: two women (a "trampy" wife and a wifely "tramp"—hardly distinguishable) side by side aboard a boat onto which they have been pushed largely by the choices of the men they love, about to be launched into an uncertain future.

6

A Night Without a Star

The Country Girl (1955)

To allow to any human beings no existence of their own but what depends on others, is giving far too high a premium on bending others to their purposes. Where liberty cannot be hoped for, and power can, power becomes the grand object of human desire. . . .

John Stuart Mill, The Subjection of Women (1869)

There were two Hollywood films released in 1955 that focused on the *wife* of the alcoholic: *The Shrike* and *The Country Girl.* Their contrasting titles indicate the ambivalence of the culture's attitude toward this female figure. A shrike is a drab bird with a sharply notched beak which impales its prey on thorns. A country girl, as Clifford Odets used the term in his screenplay, is an innocent bystander, someone pure who transcends the adulteration of earthly urban life. In more archetypal terms, these opposites translate to shrew and goddess.

Significantly, each film seeks to establish the guilt or innocence, not of the alcoholic, but of the alcoholic's wife. It is taken for granted that the alcoholic is guilty of weakness and vulnerability. What is debated, then, is whether the wife is guilty by virtue of her strength. In other words, do strong women create weak men?

In both films, the alcoholic husband is in show business. This authorial choice is made, I suspect, because show business is one area of American endeavor that has been consistently open to women as well as men. Thus, the anxiety of the weak show business husband that his strong wife is trying to encroach on his domain has a basis in reality.

But then the real question is whether the wives of these alcoholics are guilty of *ambition*, which they exercise by influencing and undermining their husbands. Both films attempt to answer the question with a simple yes or no and, consequently, each ignores the truth: that so long as ambition is adjudged sinful in a woman, she will be forced to repress it; and that repressed desires eventually surface, often in destructive ways. Neither film challenges the cultural conviction that female ambition is wicked.[1] Therefore, Odets in his exoneration of his heroine must prove that she is ambition-free.

However, director George Seaton's *The Country Girl* provides a more complex portrayal of its female protagonist than it perhaps intends: for she is revealed to be a woman of extraordinary intelligence, ability, and power who is imprisoned in a role of total self-abnegation, and whose value as a goddess is proportionate to the enormity of her self-sacrifice.

The film depicts more clearly than any other American movie in the fifties the identity abyss between male reverence and damnation above which the transitional American woman was suspended. It also faithfully reflects men's sense of themselves as an endangered species, their capitulation to a psychic exhaustion[2] which created

---

[1] Even male ambition is condemned in *The Country Girl* when the alcoholic husband loses his son while posing for a publicity photo for his record company. The male American attitude toward ambition is hopelessly ambivalent because, on the one hand, manhood is by definition ambitious; furthermore, America's economic system is based on individual ambition; on the other hand, ambition is subconsciously viewed as the root of all evil. Cf. the discussion of ambition in Chapter 1, "The Scarlet 'A.' "

[2] The wages of male supremacy are discussed in Herbert Goldberg's *The Hazards of Being Male: Surviving the Myth of Masculine Privilege* (New York: New American Library, 1977).

a power vacuum ("a night without a star") they justifiably feared women might emerge from bondage to fill.

The movie begins with a New York theatrical audition for a replacement lead in a play called *The Land Around Us*. The director, Bernie Dodd (William Holden), wants a former musical comedy star named Frank Elgin (Bing Crosby) to get the part, but when Elgin learns it is the lead, he becomes frightened and leaves the theater.

Dodd seeks him out at his "home," a furnished room above a restaurant which Frank shares with his wife, Georgie (Grace Kelly), but Elgin is not there. Dodd develops an immediate antipathy for Elgin's wife. He first patronizes her by using the word *"touché"* and then translating it. He then disparages her appearance: "You try to look like an old lady and you're not. You shouldn't wear your hair like that. There's two kinds of women. Those who pay too much attention to themselves, and those who don't pay enough." Finally, he tries to impose a conventionally ambitious identity on her by asking if she was an actress before Elgin married her. Georgie tells him, "I'm just a girl from the country. The theater and the people in it have always been a complete mystery to me. They still are." In fact, Georgie is an intellectual who reads "Dreiser, Balzac, Montaigne . . ." Bernie is predictably surprised.

Frank appears, insisting he left the theater to ask Georgie's advice about taking the part. When Dodd questions him about his drinking, Frank says that he only drank in the past because of his son's death. But he balks at accepting the role, and Georgie accuses him of being "afraid of the responsibility."

Dodd alternately flatters Elgin's ego and assures Georgie he will be a strict taskmaster with Elgin. "No pity. I like that," Georgie says. *She* negotiates the contractual arrangements with Dodd, objecting to a two-week clause, which means that Elgin can be fired at any point with only two weeks' notice. Dodd holds to that arrangement, telling Elgin, "Talk it over with your agent here."

Rehearsals begin. After a bad one, Frank hints to Dodd that he has trouble with his wife. "Oh, I know, I know," Dodd says, referring to his own bad marriage which recently ended in divorce. "They all start out as Juliets and wind up as Lady Macbeths."

Frank launches into a lengthy monologue about Georgie's emotional collapse after their son's death. He says that she became a "hopeless drunk," slit her wrists, and was jealous of his work:

> So in an effort to give her some purpose in life, I made her feel that I needed her in my work. I let her pick all the songs I should record, and the shows I ought to do. She started taking over everything then. She became very possessive and wanted to make all the decisions, had to be with me all the time. Whenever I was away from her, why, she acted as if I'd run off with another woman or something. She had fits of depression and one time she set fire to the hotel suite. That's when I began hitting the bottle pretty hard.

Elgin says Georgie quit drinking as soon as he began. At this point Georgie arrives to pick Frank up at the theater. Dodd invites them out for coffee. "She's the one who makes all the decisions in our family," Elgin says, deferring the invitation to his wife. "Is that true, Mrs. Elgin?" Bernie asks. "To the extent Frank's brought out the mother in me, yes," Georgie replies.

In a subsequent scene, Elgin's theme song is played over the radio and it recalls for him the loss of his son. In a flashback sequence, he is asked by a publicity photographer to take hold of a disc-shaped emblem of his record company, as if he is reaching out for his next hit. When he lets go of his son's hand to comply with the photographer's directive, the little boy runs in front of a car and is killed.

After this recollection, Frank begins to drink again and wants to leave Dodd's show. "I'll mess it up just like I've messed up everything else in my life," he tells Georgie. But Georgie insists Frank stay with the play, and they go to Boston for an out-of-town tryout.

Backstage in the midst of a performance, Frank angrily demands that Georgie ask Dodd for a "dresser" (someone to help him make fast costume changes) and insists also that his understudy not be permitted to skulk around backstage. But Frank's tension is magically dispelled when other actors approach him and confess their own stage fright. He is calm and reassuring. "What a wonderful guy," one of the actresses says.

After the show, Georgie approaches Dodd with Frank's demands. "If anything has to be said that might cause any antagonism, well, that's my job," Georgie explains.

Dodd becomes abusive toward her, accusing her of encouraging Frank's weakness. When Frank enters the scene, he denies that he needs a dresser or that he is bothered by the presence of his understudy, so it seems as if Georgie is fabricating demands for her own satisfaction.

The out-of-town reviews of the play are bad. Frank is said to lack authority. Dodd defends Frank to the producer of the play by insisting that Frank lacks authority "because his wife has too much of it." Georgie warns Dodd that Frank is about to go on a bender. "Why is it that women always think they understand men better than men do?" Dodd inquires acidly. "Maybe because they live with them," Georgie responds.

Dodd coerces Georgie into returning to New York and letting him handle Frank. As Georgie is preparing to leave, Frank accuses her of being involved with some man back in New York. He goes off on a drunken spree and is jailed.

When Bernie and Georgie go to bail Frank out, Bernie mentions Georgie's drinking and suicide attempt and the incident of the hotel room fire. Georgie reveals that Frank's monologue about her was derived from one of his hit plays. Bernie is repentant. Georgie confides that her only desire is to see Frank on his feet again so that she can "get out from under" and live her own life. In response, Bernie kisses her passionately. "I never knew there was such a woman," he says in awe. "Loyal, steadfast . . ."

Later, he calls Elgin "an unreliable slobbering drunk," and insists that Elgin has used his son's accident as camouflage for his own cowardice. Frank agrees: "It was good to find a respectable excuse for failure," he says, and adds that he was willing to use anything to stay at the center of attention. He concludes that it is his disgust with his own narcissistic immaturity which makes him drink.

Apparently salvaged by his confession, Frank goes on to a triumphant opening night in New York. The producer of the show comes backstage to invite Frank to a party and extend his contract. Frank accuses him of hypocrisy and demands that he remove his hat in Georgie's presence.

At the producer's party, Bernie forces Georgie to choose between him and Frank. Elgin delivers a speech of dramatic renunciation: "But, Georgie, don't dismiss what we've had together. I gave you ten of the roughest years anybody ever spent outside of a concentration camp. Could be more of the same." Then he admits he has just given a performance; he heroically bypasses a pianist playing the song that usually sends him into a guilty tailspin about his son's death and he leaves the party.

Georgie tearfully watches him go and then runs after him, leaving Bernie alone to contemplate his rave reviews.

The Country Girl is a case history of pathological symbiosis which resolves itself by "curing" half the pathology—the male half. That the film ends happily confirms that crippling *female* dependency is not regarded as pathological. On the contrary, it is Georgie's strength and assertiveness, both of which diminish as Frank resumes his role as head of the household, which are considered abnormal.

Nonetheless, the true nature of Georgie's pathology is that she can only envision herself in some spatial relation to a man, preferably *behind* him. When Bernie Dodd contemptuously presents his ex-wife's theory that "behind every great man there [is] a great woman," Georgie defends the idea with what is clearly a vested interest. In reality, though, Frank tends to stand behind *her,* as when Bernie first offers him the lead in the play.

There is a hopeful moment when Georgie tells Bernie that she would prefer to be single, if only Frank would get back on his feet again and let her "get out from under": "All I want is my own name and a modest job to buy sugar for my coffee. You can't believe that, can you? You can't believe that a woman is crazy out of her mind to live alone, in one room, by herself." But Georgie's prayer for liberation is hollow. First of all, she would have no reason to leave Frank once he was back on his feet (as the end of the film demonstrates). In addition, she is heavily dependent upon men's affirmation of her as a woman. When Bernie kisses her after her little outburst about independence, she responds breathlessly that "No one's looked at [her] as a woman in years," and she caresses her shoulders after he is gone.

If a woman needs men to make her feel like a woman, if she cannot affirm her own sexual identity, then men have the power to withhold that affirmation unless the woman behaves as they want her to. That is precisely what occurs in *The Country Girl* and what has occurred in the world at large. "You're loyal, steadfast, and devoted," Bernie tells Georgie as if he were casting a part in a play. "I like that in a woman." But Georgie is also many of the things Bernie hates. Earlier in the film, he calls her "a failure," "a frustrated female," and adds that Frank's weakness gives her "a reason for being, a feeling of power to control and manipulate someone else's life." Calling Georgie a failure clarifies how completely her fate is bound up with Frank's. She is a failure because Frank has failed. Knowing this, she tells Bernie that she wants "to do everything in [her] power to make him a success." But Frank's failure is not merely a negative reflection on Georgie; it is also an opportunity for her ambitions and abilities to surface. "I don't like to make myself obtrusive—unless, of course, Frank needs my help," she tells Bernie. In fact, she *may* not obtrude unless Frank falters. But when he does, she can use her "power" to "make" a success of him. So his weakness does indeed give her "a reason for being" and "a feeling of power" (neither of which she has when Frank is strong). And while she does not as a married woman have the liberty to control her own life, she can exercise her longing for control by directing her husband's life.

Bernie's ex-wife, whom he describes as "twisted," once told him, "I hope your next play is a flop—so the whole world can see how much I love you even though you're a failure." What she actually wanted was an opportunity to be seen and appreciated by "the whole world," something she felt she could only attain if Bernie failed. This "twisting" of women's aspirations into a desire for the downfall of men is the inevitable consequence of a man-made social

system which denies them any normal outlets for their ambitions. If they can only be powerful at men's expense, then they will have an investment in sabotaging men. Georgie finally acknowledges that she has contributed to Frank's illness by nurturing his infantilism, but she merely concludes that she cannot risk being with a weak man again, rather than that she needs to pursue a life of her own. In other words, she decides that she requires a stronger cage, a man powerful enough to keep her own power under wraps.

But strong men were not a staple of the fifties. In American plays and films of that decade, it was weak men, defeated by society and ultimately by life, who proliferated, delivering staggering confessions of inability to maintain their self-imposed burden of male supremacy. Frank Elgin's confession to Georgie is characteristic: "You

The Country Girl. Director Bernie Dodd (William Holden) tries to "breathe life into [the] corpse" of alcoholic entertainer Frank Elgin (Bing Crosby). Bernie represents the spirit of traditional American masculinity which Frank has lost.

The Country Girl. Dodd and Frank Elgin's wife, Georgie (Grace Kelly), fight for control of Georgie's husband. This power struggle is actually a battle of the sexes for dominance, which was up for grabs in the fifties as a result of American men's epidemic passivity.

don't know what it's like to stand out there on that stage all alone with the whole show on your shoulders. If I'm no good, the show's no good." *The Country Girl* strives to restore Frank's courage.

The play *The Land Around Us,* in which Frank is cast as lead, is a metaphor for the America our mythical forefathers created, and it establishes the discrepancy between that institutional male ethic and the vulnerable, frightened, guilty, often childish men of the fifties who attempted to preserve it. It also reveals a discrepancy between the traditional woman, who is depicted as a cheerful shadow of support, and "new" women like Georgie, who are critics. Bernie tells Georgie that she cannot be both a critic and a wife, and he instructs her on how she *ought* to behave by describing how he will handle Frank once she is sent back to New York:

> I'll begin by not calling him a cunning drunkard. I'll give
> him pride and confidence by occasionally *rejoicing* in his God-
> given talents instead of constantly reminding him of his weak-
> ness. I'll let him face a decision without first filling him full
> of doubts and fears and I won't stifle him with my own
> inadequacy and bitterness. I might have to bend the truth
> here and there but I'll get a performance out of him.

These instructions on how to "get a performance out of" a man,
how to keep him going in an exploitative relationship, are put forth
to preserve the traditional masculine and feminine roles. Bernie
also knows how to "get a performance out of" Georgie, and that is
to worship her, as Frank once did ("Isn't mommy a doll?" he asked
his son Johnny before the accident), for her womanly beauty and
wifely dedication.

Frank's alcoholism demands a different performance on Georgie's
part, one which Bernie perceives as perilous because it permits
Georgie to be dominant. Frank takes the place of his own dead child
and Georgie becomes the motherly drudge (Georgie the martyr) who
cannot leave him until he grows up. But Frank, in regressing to
childhood, surrenders all responsibility to Georgie (his theme song
is "You've Got What It Takes to Take Me"), which releases him and
permits her to play at being the man of the house, "little George."
And although being the wife of an actor who "hates himself," who
would "do or say anything to be liked by others," who has given
her "ten of the roughest years anybody ever spent outside of a
concentration camp" is "not the easiest of jobs," it is a job, a challenge, of the same sort which attracts Bernie. He wants to "breathe
life into [the] corpse" of Frank Elgin. He competes with Georgie
for the right to control Frank's destiny. "I'm warning you," he tells
Georgie, "I'm going to fight you as hard as I can for this man," and
later he tells Frank, "If we go on together, you move in with me."

This competition between a man and a woman over the right to
"control and manipulate someone else's life" is ultimately a fierce
competition for the male role itself, the right to power, which Frank,
the typical American man of the fifties, has abandoned and which is

therefore up for grabs. The contest appears to end in a draw, but the movie actually gives victory to the men.

Bernie admits he cannot handle Frank (he doesn't really want to have to *care* for another man) and tosses that traditional responsibility back at Georgie. But it is Bernie who confronts Frank with the truth that his son's accident is merely an excuse for Frank to regress to a manipulative, narcissistic infant. And it is this truth which jars Frank back into a tentative male adulthood. At the same time, Bernie's amorous attentions restore Georgie to her "femininity"— the pretty, passive doll's existence she led before the accident which killed her son. So while Bernie does not win outright possession of either Frank or Georgie, he restores the traditional male and female roles, which is his real function in the drama.

Bernie is a sort of masculine essence: powerful, aloof, alternately misogynistic and adoring of women as idealized goddesses. His play about the American male ideal, his desire to restore Frank to his manhood, and his verbal jousts with Georgie (St. George vs. St. Georgie, each perceiving the other as the dragon) which begin with the word *"touché,"* make it clear that his importance to the story is largely emblematic and mechanical (in the sense of deus ex machina, the magical resolver of conflict). That such an abstract, elemental male is called in to do battle with a mere female suggests the degree of anxiety men felt about women in the fifties.

Georgie is largely unaware of the threat she poses ("How could you be so angry at someone you didn't even know?" she asks Bernie) and of her freedom to emerge from the imprisoning shelter of a male-dominated world. But her potential is nonetheless obvious in the film (Grace Kelly won an Oscar for her performance). There is one instance in particular which presents Georgie on the brink of awesome emergence. She walks regally onto the vacant stage which the cast of the play has abandoned for the evening, looks out into the darkness at the sea of empty seats, and says, "There is nothing quite so mysterious and silent as a dark theater. A night without a star." Her husband has yet to become the star that will illuminate that shadowy cavern, and so she momentarily fills the void, emitting an eerie, chilling radiance which stuns Bernie into silence. This dazzling episode suggests not only what lies within her but the inevitability of its emergence, either as destructive energy within the confines of a repressive female role, or in some healthier, freer, future form.

7

The Eleven-Year Itch

The Tender Trap (1955)

Few women would want to thumb their noses at husbands, children, and community and go off on their own. Those who do may be talented individuals, but they rarely are successful women.

Redbook *Magazine* (1960)

The title of *The Tender Trap* is an apt illustration of the unacknowledged ambivalence of the fifties, in that the contradictory terms sit together alliteratively as if they were perfectly mated. The contradiction exists but it is artfully obscured. Love, the title song explains, is the tender trap, but the movie is about marriage, not love. In fact, there is virtually no love at all in *The Tender Trap*. Significantly enough, there is also no marriage. Marriage occurs off-screen, in Indianapolis, or in photographs of dour-looking parents or as a wistfully outlined goal. The story takes place in a nether world between bachelorhood and marriage, a purgatorial passage with heaven and hell at interchangeable ends, depending upon one's point of view from moment to moment.

Charlie Reader (Frank Sinatra), a New York theatrical agent, has a harem of devoted female playmates (Poppy, Jessica, Helen, and Sylvia). His best friend Joe (David Wayne) comes to stay with him, temporarily escaping from an exhausted eleven-year marriage in Indiana. Charlie believes in marriage in principle. Joe in practice no longer does.

Joe meets Sylvia (Celeste Holm), the most interesting member of Charlie's harem, and falls in love with her. Charlie meets Julie (Debbie Reynolds), a talented young bud who is proceeding toward marriage like a robot, and falls in love with her. But when Charlie refuses to marry her, she rejects him (her wedding deadline is March 29th, the date of her parents' anniversary) and Charlie, on the rebound, becomes engaged to Sylvia, who is thirty-three and desperate.

Then Julie reappears and Charlie becomes engaged to her. When the two fiancées confront each other, Sylvia bows out nobly. That is Joe's cue to propose to Sylvia, but she turns him down, explaining that she merely reminds him of his wife, whom she insists she resembles, and that she doesn't love him. However, as she is leaving she asks, "Where were you eleven years ago?" which suggests that she may be in love with him after all, and only feigning rejection to save his marriage. Nonetheless, in the elevator she meets for the first time the man she will marry in the next scene. Joe returns to his wife. And Charlie reunites with Julie at Sylvia's wedding. In the final sequence, all four of the happy people rejoin to sing the theme song against a boundless blue horizon.

The movie's ostensible burden is to convince its male characters that marriage is better than romance. The *hidden* burden of the film is to persuade its female *audience* that marriage is all that matters. Consequently, we are presented with an unlikely world in which talented and successful women are caricaturishly obsessed with marriage and where a man can become sufficiently panicked by one dateless night to propose twice. Where obsession and panic reign, love is beside the point. The film repeatedly corroborates this, although it eventually contradicts itself.

After Joe gets a glimpse of Charlie's bachelor paradise, he asks, "What have you got?" Charlie replies that it's what he hasn't got that counts, and what he hasn't got is a wife. Thus, we are not meant to see Charlie as an extraordinary fellow with sensational sex appeal (i.e., Charlie is not Frank Sinatra, although Sinatra plays the part) but as an ordinary fellow from Indiana—in other words, like any man in the film audience. His appeal to women is strictly circumstantial. Poppy, an editor at Doubleday, Jessica, a buyer for the largest chain of women's fashion stores in the South, and Sylvia, a violinist in the NBC symphony orchestra, all want to marry him because he's single. Sylvia explains their position in the following monologue:

> We come to this town from Springfield and Des Moines and Fort Worth and Salt Lake City. We're young, we're pretty, and we're talented. All we have to do to get married is stay home. But the boys back home don't have what we want. We've got our eyes on something else. A career! Glamour! Excitement! And this is the place to find it. So we come to New York. And we do pretty well. Not great but—pretty well. We make a career. We find the excitement and the glamour. We go to first nights. We buy little mink stoles. Headwaiters call us by name. It's fun. Wonderful. Till one fine day we look around and we're thirty-three years old, we haven't got a man . . . Joe, do you have any idea what's available to a woman thirty-three? Married men, drunks, pretty boys looking for someone to support them, lunatics looking for their fifth divorce. Quite a list, isn't it. So we set our cap for Charlie! He's eligible, he's attractive, he's employed, and reasonably sane.

Joe interrupts with the question, "But you don't love him, do you?" Sylvia replies, "How did the word love ever creep into this conversation?"

Sylvia holds the false expectation that a career or a marriage should provide total personal fulfillment. Moreover, she misperceives the very nature of these two phenomena, describing them both as things one has, static and unspecified objects. As such, she can conceive of them as mutually exclusive absolutes, and if one fails to provide total gratification, she can turn to the other—as she is now turning from career to marriage.

This reduction of career, specifically, to the level of a nonentity with fringe benefits (little mink stoles, etc.) is consistent with the depiction of men's careers in the film as well. We have little sense of the reality of Charlie's job as a theatrical agent except for a few brief scenes when he meets Julie (a fringe benefit); and in these scenes he is frustrated, first by Julie's refusal to sign a standard contract and then by Julie's failure to attend a rehearsal because she has been mesmerized by the attractions of a Home Show. Joe's job is never mentioned and therefore forms no part of his reality or our conception of him. These distortions and omissions (by no means confined to this film) hint at a *general* dislocation of identity and satisfaction from one's workaday endeavors. If so, the negative presentation of women's careers (with the concomitant glorification of domestic life) might, at least in part, be a reflection of a genuinely felt male negativity about work itself, a sense of meaningless anonymity as a wage earner, rather than a conspiracy to keep women away from potentially joyful pursuits.

At the end of Joe's conversation with Sylvia, he insists that there are worse things for a girl than not getting married. But when Sylvia demands that he "name three," he is silent. Neither Joe nor the film is willing to admit openly that a bad marriage might be worse, but there are hints: when Joe describes his marriage to Ethel as a mandatory parade of fencing lessons and braces for the children, obedience school for the dog, and wall-to-wall carpeting for the home; when he reports a phone conversation with Ethel in which she, as a consequence of being "restless and bored," has decided to carpet the bathroom; when Joe suggests to Julie that what fulfills women (marriage) may not fulfill men; and when Charlie (and the film audience) confront photographs of Julie's parents, the father bald, the mother fat, and both unhappy-looking. But Julie's response to Joe and Charlie is meant to cancel out these grim shadows. Marriage, Julie says, will fulfill *her* man.

In other words, unhappiness may be a feature of other people's marriages, but it won't be a part of hers. She's different. Joe, a casualty of a conventional middle-class marriage, still believes this as much as Julie. That is why he proposes to Sylvia. But Sylvia outlines the paradox:

I want wall-to-wall carpeting, French provincial furniture, and a houseful of kids all with good straight teeth. What did you think? Moonbeams? Candlelight suppers? Cloud number seven? Joe, you know what you've got? You've got the married man's dream. You want a girl. That's what you all want—a girl. And that's what you can never have. Because the only way to have a girl is not to marry her. Because then she becomes a wife. That's something entirely different.

"No, Sylvia," Joe says, "you'd be different." The truth is that Sylvia probably would be different, and that Ethel—so bored and restless —might be different, too, if marriage allowed for individual differences and did not presume to fulfill one's entire life. However, Sylvia accepts the traditional picture of marriage that Ethel is living out and that Julie is scheming to achieve. "A career is just fine but it's no substitute for marriage," Julie says, quite rightly. But the combination of marriage *and* career for women is never once whispered in the film. Sylvia says, "I guess I'll go on fiddling until I die or get married, whichever comes first." The film conceives of marriage as a dead-end absolute, with career, freedom, and romance at the other end of the spectrum. As in death, a woman can't take them with her.

Moreover, there is the problem of "mating"—that is, how choices of marital partners get made. The film has everything from "puppy" love—Ethel's high school romance with Joe and Helen's engagement to a poodle owner she meets while walking Charlie's dog—to no love at all: Sylvia's marriage to the stranger in the elevator, or Poppy's acceptance of a boyfriend who, although a "square" with plans for Radio City Music Hall and "afterwards, if it's not too late, Schrafft's," can be depended upon to call her the next day, unlike Charlie. But ideally, there is "falling in love," and "falling in love" is heaven. Not only do we see the film's major characters up against a blue sky at the end, but Charlie specifically tells us so:

> You know my idea of heaven now, Joe? To be so much in love with a girl, and to have her love you so much that you wouldn't think of taking a vacation from each other for eleven years. Eleven years!

Words matter, even in a movie, and falling into heaven makes as much sense as a tender trap. In fact, trap and falling are equated in the film. Joe warns Charlie against Julie: "Stay away from this girl. She's a trap with the trigger all set." Immediately after, he reminds Charlie of his boyhood habit of falling out of treehouses.

The treehouse signifies two opposite ideas in the film: first, Charlie's idyllic boyhood, his male independence (a kind of heaven, up in a tree, which is represented by Charlie's appearance, alone, at the beginning of the film up against a clear blue sky); and second, the domesticity which Charlie evades. From this second perspective, Charlie is a fallen man or, in the parlance of the film, a stinker and a louse. Julie wants to reform him by marriage. And Joe, although warning Charlie against falling in love with Julie (i.e., falling out of his bachelor boy's treehouse), subsequently calls him "one of the few indecent men I've ever met" and suggests that he redeem himself by marrying Sylvia. Thus, the film proposes that Charlie must fall (lose one kind of heaven) to be redeemed from being a fallen man (for evading another kind of heaven). That may make sense in one of John Donne's metaphysical poems, but in a Hollywood movie it reads more like a contradiction than a paradox. In fact, "heavenly" marriage is inadvertently depicted as a kind of punishment which makes a man holy, a bad-tasting medicine which renders him well. He can either rationalize this unfortunate situation, like the devil in *Paradise Lost,* who through spurious logic proceeds to the conclusion that hell is better than heaven, or he can become irrational by "falling in love" and genuinely mistake hell (marriage) for heaven. Charlie's two engagements represent these two choices, just as Charlie's two appearances in heaven, at the beginning of the film as a bachelor, and at the end as a husband, equate these opposing states.

However, the film, not satisfied with the equation, attempts to discredit bachelorhood and establish the superiority of marriage. Since it cannot prove by direct demonstration that marriage is more heavenly than single life, it operates according to a simple syllogism:

Single life looks like heaven
but it can be lonely.

The Tender Trap. Marriage-obsessed Julie (Debbie Reynolds) has play-boy bachelor Charlie (Frank Sinatra) try out a chair she is thinking of buying for her as-yet nonexistent home in Scarsdale, for her as-yet non-existent husband and children. Ironically, her powerful managerial in-stincts are focused on creating a life for herself in which she will have to suppress her aggressiveness.

> So I reject heaven for marriage
> WHICH PROVES that marriage is even
> more heavenly than bachelorhood.

The same syllogism is applied to the women, all relatively successful, independent people who, out of loneliness, opt for marriage, which again "proves" the superiority of marriage over even the most glam-orous and romantic single life.

Billy Wilder uses the syllogism again in *The Seven-Year Itch* (1957) when the Tom Ewell character rejects the advances of Marilyn Monroe (not just any pretty girl) to return to his mundane marriage. In addition, the syllogism renders the seven-, or eleven-year itch—which is a source of both films' anxieties—a positive event; not the indication of boredom and dissatisfaction, fading physical attraction and the lack of real compatibility which it probably is, but, rather, a minor affliction from which a man recovers firmly reconvinced of the viability of his marital commitment.

Both films function for the audience as inoculations. We get a dose of romance to immunize us against the temptation of the real thing outside the movie theater. Or at the very least, we get to cheat vicariously by having our romance while still remaining sanctimonious about the superiority of marriage and fidelity. Moral superiority is important to the characters in both films. Charlie and Joe are mutually outraged by one another's behavior, and the Tom Ewell character in *The Seven-Year Itch* suffers endless psychological and cinematic abuse for the mere carnal contemplation of Marilyn Monroe. Thus, we are even vicariously judged and punished for our voyeuristic participation.

A peculiar characteristic of *The Tender Trap*'s position is that serious courtship, marriage, and fidelity are upheld as good regardless of the people involved. Joe belongs with Ethel because he is married to her, even though he has ceased to love her. And Charlie and Julie belong together because they are Charlie and Julie—the hero and the heroine, the cute couple, with rhymed name endings. We are meant to disregard what Julie tells Charlie after he attempts to seduce her:

> Do you think that's such a wonderful thing? Being in love with you? I never wanted to. I don't want to now. You're selfish, you're arrogant, you're spoiled, you're much too old for me. . . . Oh, lord knows why I love you, but I do.

We must not wonder whether Cinderella would be happily married to a prince, or whether Julie, a maniacal bourgeoise, will be content with Charlie, a promiscuous playboy. As long as the shoe fits . . .

But Julie, unlike Cinderella, has no fairy godmother, and must therefore scheme to get her man. This scheming ingenue is a staple of the fifties. She is one of the secretaries in *Three Coins in a Fountain* (1954)—the one with the ponytail who plots to marry the Italian prince; the debutante in *To Catch a Thief* (1955); the secretary in *Ask Any Girl* (1959), to name only a few, and she is also the villain of *All About Eve* (1950), although in *Eve* marriage is subordinated to career, which makes her ruthless energy condemnable by fifties' standards. What all these characters have in common is a lack of identity; their goal becomes a ferociously pursued substitute for identity. The Julie-type is one example of the transitional woman, an embodiment of all the contradictory needs and longings her sex was experiencing acutely for the first time in the fifties.

The scene in which Julie and Charlie "seduce" each other is a blueprint of the conflicts. "Look," Julie tells Charlie:

> I know this is the atomic age and we're two civilized adults. You made that clear. But a girl still doesn't like to call for a man at his apartment. Or meet him at a bar. Especially when the whole evening has been planned without any consultation. . . . Every date we've had has been all figured out by you. You've never asked me once, not once, what I wanted to do.

Julie foregoes the role of "civilized adult" by referring to herself as "a girl." She objects to meeting Charlie here and there for a date because it is a violation of traditional courtship, but she wants to have an equal say in planning the evening, which is the prerogative of a liberated woman.

Charlie apologizes to Julie and asks her what she wants to do. She falters. "Well, I don't know. . . . Gee, I don't know. What do you want . . . well . . ." Finally, Charlie takes over and describes the evening. Julie says, "Charlie . . . next time I tell you I want to plan an evening, just don't listen." Charlie agrees to ignore her. "Because you," she continues, "know more about how to please a lady than any other man on the Eastern seaboard." If this were as far as the scene went, it would be a typical example of a Hollywood male screenwriter's joke: give the woman a choice and she can't make up her mind. But the scene proceeds.

Julie tries to read Charlie's mail while he is changing clothes for the evening, a passive attempt at gaining power and control. Then she becomes bored at the nightclub he has selected, a kind of passive revenge for his ease in selecting it, and casually hints that her parents are away from home for the weekend. When they reach her apartment, she tells Charlie to leave—on behalf of her parents. But then she entices him to stay with the offer of a nightcap and agrees to neck with him. When his necking becomes nibbling, she tries to distract him with television and picture books. She pretends to succumb to his embrace, simultaneously looting his pocket of phone messages from other women. In a rage over her discovery of his rampant promiscuity, she presents him with an ultimatum: "You listen to me! Will you listen to me! Listen to me, God's gift to women, and listen good!" After struggling with Charlie for power in the traditional coy, sly, and passive-aggressive ways ascribed to the female, she finally asserts herself definitively, demanding that he listen to her, although she earlier told him not to pay any attention to her. After gaining his ear, she presents him with a list of her demands. He is to pick her up at her apartment, meet her folks, bring her flowers and candy, drop all other women, and ask her how she wants to spend an evening—the very right she waived earlier. Her final coup is to reverse her former compliment to him by saying that he has a lot to learn about women, and that she's going to try to make *a man* out of him. Then she indirectly proposes to him, and he indignantly refuses her. "I know a girl who comes a lot closer to my idea of being a wife than you do." With this phrase, Charlie betrays the same misconception that Julie has about finding a mate. They both have "ideas" of the people they want to marry, and they are looking for realizations of prefabricated notions, rather than individual human beings with whom they would be happy.

In a final flurry of confusion, Julie walks out on Charlie before she realizes that they are in *her* apartment and *he* should leave. But despite her confusions and contradictions, due to the fluctuations in morality during the fifties ("Does she or doesn't she?") and the alterations in appropriate courtship behavior (one must be sophisticated, but still feminine, assertive but not overbearing), Julie acts throughout the scene from a position of power, demanding her rights, relinquishing them, reclaiming them, delivering ultimatums, making demands, proposing, and finally ejecting Charlie from her apartment. Her "plan" to marry is comic precisely because it makes the man, whoever he turns out to be, almost irrelevant. She is shown picking out furniture for "her" home and she has long ago decided on the number of children she will have and where they will go to school (Scarsdale). Such independence and calculation are incompatible with a goal which, by its nature, ends independence and the opportunity to exercise authority. Such energy is misdirected, and one can easily imagine the destructive dimensions it will assume when it is trapped within a conventional Scarsdale marriage.

Celeste Holm's Sylvia, another type of transitional woman, belongs to the statistical category of professional women who married in the fifties at a higher rate than ever before. In the early sixties, one of those women, fed up and disillusioned, wrote a book entitled *The Feminine Mystique.*

8

Dogs Like Us

Marty (1955)

By 1950, . . . the average woman married at twenty, bore her last child at twenty-six, and had a life expectancy of sixty-five years. Even if she remained at home until her children were grown, she still had at least 20 years of life at home without children.
Lois W. Banner, Women in Modern America: A Brief History (1974)

M*arty,* winner of the Academy Award for Best Picture of 1955, is a liberating experience. Its major dynamic is the triumph of its two main characters over a number of crippling limitations. The film, moreover, has the delightful audacity to cast its love story (adapted by Paddy Chayefsky from his television comedy-drama) about two homely losers with actors who are genuinely homely—a departure from Hollywood tradition. Finally, it is a small-screen, black-and-white movie in a decade of Cinemascope color extravaganzas. In the midst of all this good-natured liberal rebellion, it is easy to overlook an underlying short-sightedness and conservatism; or once aware of that, to deny the film's liberal virtues; but in fact *Marty* is an amalgam of contrary impulses.

Marty (Ernest Borgnine) is a thirty-four-year-old Italian Catholic butcher and overweight bachelor who lives in New York with his widowed mother. Everyone nags him to get married, which he would gladly do if he could find a woman who wanted him.

He and his pal Angie go to the Stardust Ballroom in the hope of meeting girls, and there Marty encounters Clara (Betsy Blair). She has been brought to the ballroom by a blind date who is sufficiently disappointed in her to offer Marty, and then another man, five dollars to take her off his hands and escort her home. Marty refuses, but he follows Clara when she runs out of the ballroom in humiliation and comforts her in her rejection by telling her about his own. "Dogs like us, we ain't such dogs as we think we are."

Both people share their longings with one another. Marty wants to buy the butcher shop in which he works. Clara, a twenty-nine-year-old high school chemistry teacher, wants to take a job in Port Chester, New York, as the head of a science department. Each encourages the other to take the risk. In Clara's case, that would necessitate moving away from her parents' apartment.

Marty invites Clara home with him so that he can pick up more money. On the way, two men friends in a car with three nurses try to convince Marty to ditch Clara and join them, but Marty declines. At the house, Marty tries to kiss Clara and is momentarily rebuffed. But Clara reassures him that she likes him very much and hopes to see him again. Marty's mother, Teresa, returns home and regales them with a synopsis of what turns out to be the film's subplot: Teresa's widowed sister is creating havoc in the small apartment of her son, Thomas, and her daughter-in-law, Virginia, by refusing to relinquish her role as wife, mother, and boss of the household. She's only fifty-six years old, she tells Teresa. "What am I going to do with myself? I've got strength in my hands. I want to clean. I want to cook. I want to make dinner for my children." Virginia insists, with her husband's guilty consent, that the mother, Katarina, go live with sister Teresa and Marty. To begin with, Teresa is sympathetic to Thomas and Virginia's plight, but when Katarina warns her that the same fate will befall her when Marty gets married, she becomes frightened and sides with Katarina.

As a result, she and Clara enter into a disagreement about where a mother-in-law should live, which Marty interrupts by taking Clara home. Angie intercepts them, angry at Marty for leaving him alone at the ballroom and jealous that his friend has met a woman. When his offer to ride with Marty and Clara on the bus is rejected, he storms off. Marty promises to call Clara to confirm a date for the following evening.

The next morning, Sunday, Katarina arrives, delivered by her son Thomas, who is so tormented by guilt that he has a bitter fight with his wife and tells Marty that he is a fool to want to take on the responsibility of owning a butcher shop or to ever consider getting married. After Mass, Marty's mother delivers a diatribe against Clara, insisting that she's old, not pretty, not proper (she came to Marty's house unchaperoned), and not Italian. Later, Angie tells Marty that Clara is "a dog" who looks at least fifty years old.

Marty's intention to call Clara is derailed by these negative reactions. We see Clara forlornly sitting at home with her parents that night watching *The Ed Sullivan Show*. In the meantime Marty is once again swallowed up into the nihilistic boredom of his buddies: "What do you feel like doing tonight?" "I don't know, Ange, what do you feel like doing?" Finally he realizes that he genuinely cares about Clara, and in the last shot of the film, we see him in a phone booth calling her.

It is characteristic of the contradictory fifties that in the same year when the female characters of *The Tender Trap* want nothing more than to abandon their careers for marriage, the heroine of *Marty* can have an ambition other than marriage (although it is modest enough) and that she can look critically upon women who have given up everything of their own for the sake of their husbands and children.

There are other significant instances of emancipation in the film as well, not the least of which is Marty's rejection of "the boys" for the company of a woman. Marty's insecure pals live in a fantasy world of *Playboy* centerfolds and Mickey Spillane exploits. Mickey Spillane, a fellow named Ralph explains with awe, "knows how to handle women." Clearly "the boys" do not, so out of fear they band

Marty. Clara (Betsy Blair) and Marty (Ernest Borgnine) are the homely protagonists of a gently comic romance based on mutual respect and tenderness rather than the usual Hollywood ingredients of glamour and sexual charisma.

together and confront women in groups of two or three. Marty is the only man in the film who spends any time alone with a woman.

In addition to being afraid of women, these "boys" are elaborately and exquisitely bored with one another. Rather than a Hemingway idyll of male camaraderie, screenwriter Paddy Chayefsky gives us a comic nightmare of permanent psychic entrapment in a high school locker room.

The fact that Marty must abandon both "the boys" and his mama to pursue Clara signals that this relationship, upon which all the optimism of the film rests, is a product of *maturity*. And it is a consequence of the couple's maturity (they are both middle-aged by the teenage marriage criteria of the fifties) that they can appreciate one another's value and perceive each other's intrinsic beauty, thereby transcending the callow standards of sexual attractiveness which have rendered them both lonely losers for most of their lives.

There are, moreover, a number of other small and subtle examples of rebellion against norms in *Marty*. For example, Marty admits to Clara that he cries all the time, and that he has contemplated suicide. When Clara stops Marty from kissing her, she explains: "I just didn't feel like it, that's all," and afterward admits she doesn't know how to handle the situation. Then, without being coy, she tells Marty how much she likes him and is not ashamed to say that she wants to see him again, without waiting for him to declare his intentions first.

There is also a wonderful background vignette in which two old ladies in a bar gossip about a woman who defied the advice of her doctor by giving birth to a seventh baby. Unfortunately, the woman died. This frames the film's general attitude toward the mother-martyr who gives up everything, including her life, for her children. Clara tells Teresa, "Well, I don't think a mother should depend so much upon her children for her rewards in life."

Teresa's reply, however, introduces the conservative inertia of the society which the film's optimistic momentum attempts to ignore. "Well, that's what they teach you in New York University? In real life, it no work out like this. You wait until *you* are a mother."

The film encourages us to believe that Clara will somehow avoid the pitfalls of marriage which have overwhelmed women of a different generation like Teresa and Katarina. But Virginia, Thomas's young wife, does not seem destined for any brighter future. And how likely is it that Clara will even continue to teach once she marries Marty, let alone pursue her ambition to become the head of a high school science department?

Marty. Marty's aunt Katarina and mother, Teresa, two middle-aged Italian widows, discuss the prospect of being idle for the next twenty years of their lives. Katerina lives with her son and daughter-in-law, who want to run their own household. She warns that the same fate will befall Teresa when Marty marries. They exemplify the plight of women whose only function in life is to serve husbands and children.

Similarly, the film promotes acceptance of the courtship ritual, despite its injuries to the spirit and self-esteem of its participants, simply because Marty and Clara eventually transcend its humiliations.

If "liberal" films have fallen into disrepute, it is because they overestimate the power of individual transcendence and thereby avoid the threat of radical social revision. Clara is as much at the mercy of Marty's prerogative to pursue or abandon their relationship as any less "liberated" woman. We see this clearly in the scene where she tearfully awaits his long overdue phone call. But because Marty is merciful, and because the men in the film are depicted as vulnerable and helpless victims of their apprehensions and pretensions, it *seems* as though his prerogative is not power.

When we watch Marty at the beginning of the film call Mary

Feeny, a girl he met in a movie theater a month before, for a date; when we listen to him humbly attempt to remind her who he is ("I'm the stocky one, the heavyset fellow"); when we see him wilt under the disappointment of her rejection and cry out afterward to his mother, "Whatever it is that women like, I ain't got it!"—it is virtually impossible to remember that he has the advantage over Mary Feeny, and that while she can reject him, she cannot violate the boundaries of her female passivity by calling *him*, or any other man, for a date. This is equally true of the ballroom scene, where a male wallflower like Marty has the power, with persistence, to remedy his situation, while the female wallflowers, like Clara, can only sit and wait—or run away.

We are appalled when Clara's date trades her to another man for a five-dollar bribe. But the rationale for palming her off on another man is an inherent part of the traditional date, in which a man "purchases" a woman for the evening by paying her way.

Money is power, and while a great many men have assumed the financial responsibility for a date without harboring ulterior motives, other men have come to consider it a license for various kinds of aggressive behavior, particularly after the reason for the custom—women's unemployment and unequal financial status—evaporated.

Marty pays Clara's way—although Clara is a working woman and is perfectly capable of paying for herself. In fact, he would be insulted if it dawned on Clara to assert her financial independence. His pride is contingent upon her willingness to assume a symbolically subordinate role.

Moreover, as nice as Marty is, he feels entitled to "a lousy kiss" later in the evening because he has, out of consideration for Clara's feelings, passed up an opportunity to join his buddies in a car full of nurses: "money in the bank," as one fellow called them; that is, a sure source of sexual gratification. The *language* of this expression suggests that for these men a date is a financial transaction in which they expect a sexual return. As Mark Schorer writes in the introduction to the Riverside edition (1956) of *Pride and Prejudice*:

> When moral and emotional situations are persistently expressed

in economic figures ("he was longing to publish his prosperous love"), we can hardly escape the recognition that this is a novel about marriage as a market, and about the female as marketable.

The film *Marty* satirizes this mercantile attitude without acknowledging its power to justify a variety of male actions from rape to wife beating to the trading of one's date to another man as if she were one's property to dispose of as one liked. But perhaps the movie did all it could at the time.

Schorer, outlining the sociopolitical limitations of *Pride and Prejudice*—a novel in which two individuals transcend the shortcomings of their respective milieux and attain the possibility of an exceptional matrimonial felicity within a larger spectrum of marital failure—explains that "For all its implicit and expressed judgments on society, *Pride and Prejudice* is by no means a novel that will entertain any notions of rejecting it. . . . Ultimately, what had been the feudal order was to be engulfed by what was growing into the mercantile order, but in the exact time that she was writing and from her country perspective, Jane Austen can hardly be expected to tell us this in so many words, although she already dramatizes the process." These astute observations are, I believe, equally applicable in principle to Paddy Chayevsky's modest comedy. *Marty* recorded an alteration in the status of women in relation to men, marriage, and children as it was occurring, without its makers fully realizing the ultimate implications of this alteration, or advocating an overthrow of what was perceived in the middle of the fifties to be an inevitable sexual hierarchy.

9

Oppression in Sheep's Clothing

All That Heaven Allows *(1956)*

We women grow to think that because we are wanted as lovers, wives, and mothers, it might be because we are wanted as human beings. But if by chance or natural inclination we attempt to move outside these male-defined and male-dependent roles, we find that they are, in reality, barriers.

Betty Roszak, *"The Human Continuum"*
Masculine/Feminine: Readings in Sexual Mythology
and the Liberation of Women *(1969)*

Douglas Sirk's elegant melodrama *All That Heaven Allows,* like D. H. Lawrence's *Lady Chatterley's Lover,* is a declaration of social and sexual protest in the form of a seduction of a conventional woman by a natural man. Despite its glossy postcard appearance, the movie glorifies counterculture values that hearken back to America's archetypal individualist, Henry David Thoreau, and forward to the leftist uprising of the late sixties. But while the film liberates its heroine from self-sacrificing motherhood, a passionless widowhood, and a stifling suburban community, its protest against the fifties bourgeoisie is ultimately reactionary, betraying a nostalgia for the past, rather than a hunger for a better future.

This nostalgia, which also informed social aspects of the political revolution in the sixties, urges civil disobedience and the revitalization of the *traditional* male and female roles through a return to an agrarian and craft economy where men can be self-sufficient individuals in harmony with nature, and women can make a more substantial contribution to the economic welfare of the family:

> In the past, whether a woman lived on a farm, a Dutch city in the seventeenth century, or a colonial town in the eighteenth century, women in all strata of society except the very top were never able to be full-time mothers as the twentieth century middle class American woman has become. These women were productive members of farm and craft teams along with their farmer, baker, or printer husbands and other adult kin. . . . These women were not lonely because the world came into their homes in the form of customers, clients, or patients in villages and towns, or farm hands and relatives on the farm; such women had no reason to complain of the boredom and solitude of spending ten-hour days alone with babies and young children because their days were peopled with adults.[1]

Such a productive and vital past seems like an inviting alternative for the heroine of *All That Heaven Allows,* whose heritage as a twentieth-century American woman is "boredom and solitude." It is difficult to imagine a woman who has less identity and purpose than she. Apparently without a single interest in life beyond the well-being of her children, she is a warm and charming blank, waiting (now that her husband has died) to re-attach herself to life through some new man. It therefore seems like an act of mercy to offer her not merely passionate romance but a rustic world where meaningful identity and function are provided for women by the life choices of men. In just this way, the audience, along with the

---

[1] Alice S. Rossi, "Equality Between the Sexes: An Immodest Proposal," *The Woman in America,* ed. Robert Jay Lifton (Boston: Beacon Press, 1967).

heroine, is seduced, to the extent that it fails to realize such a rescue of the present by the *past* evades the necessity of women's social and emotional emancipation in the *future*.[2]

Throughout the fifties and well into the present, this seductive soft-sell has been used to introduce all manner of *apparently progressive* alternatives to women in American films [3] in order to prevent them from perceiving the obvious one: an existence not necessarily separate from, but *independent of*, men, with equal status, freedom, and privilege. Women have, instead, been encouraged to

> swim vigorously *with the tides of life,* rather than lie helplessly tossed about bemoaning their handicaps as women, or rather than try to "rise above" the pressures on them in the typical male fashion. Such a strong embrace of the female lifestyle would seem to offer a promising way of life to the "feminist" who wants to stay feminine and yet leave her mark. Men may build greater monuments—particularly to themselves—but how long do monuments last *sub specie aeternitatis*? [4]

---

[2] Women radicals in the late sixties were dismayed to discover that men's leftist politics did not alter their perception of women's status. Marlene Dixon commented in "The Rise of Women's Liberation" (*Ramparts* magazine, 1969) that "although [women] constitute a potential mass base for the radical movement, in terms of movement priorities they are ignored; indeed they might as well be invisible. Far from being an accident, this omission is a direct outgrowth of the solid male supremist beliefs of white radical and left-liberal men." Robin Morgan, in an editorial in *Rat: Subterranean News* (1970), an underground newspaper which "lent" itself to feminist women radicals for a week, referred to "the male-dominated peace movement" and instructed her sisters to say good-bye "to Hip Culture and the so-called Sexual Revolution, which has functioned toward women's freedom as did the Reconstruction toward former slaves—reinstituted oppression by another name."
[3] Like Robin Morgan, Betty Friedan in *The Feminine Mystique* questions the Sexual Revolution as a genuine source of women's liberation: "Sex is the only frontier open to women who have always lived within the confines of the feminine mystique. In the past fifteen years, the sexual frontier has been forced to expand perhaps beyond the limits of possibility, to fill the time available, to fill the vacuum created by denial of larger goals and purposes for American women."
[4] David C. McClelland, "Wanted: A New Self-Image for Women," *The Woman in America,* ed. Robert J. Lifton (Boston: Beacon Press, 1967).

All That Heaven Allows. This predominantly silhouetted shot obscures the age difference between Ron (Rock Hudson) and Carrie (Jane Wyman) while clearly establishing Ron's dominance in the relationship. He wants Carrie to abandon her empty middle-class widowhood for a spiritually richer, rustic life with him.

Molly Haskell, seduced along with everyone else in this instance, praises *All That Heaven Allows* in her book *From Reverence to Rape* for having the heroine choose "the greater happiness over the lesser happiness" by casting her lot with a passionate, iconoclastic tree farmer. Haskell fails to acknowledge that this choice is *not* all that heaven allows, as it pretends to be. Nor is it all that a woman may need.

The movie begins outdoors in suburban New York in autumn with a dialogue between Carrie Scott (Jane Wyman), the widow, and Sarah (Agnes Moorehead), her best friend, about who might accompany Carrie to dinner at "the club." There's Tom Allenby. But "he's forty," Sarah explains, "which means he'll consider any female over eighteen too old. We might as well face it." And then there's Harvey. "At least he's available." In the background, pruning Carrie's trees, is Ron Kirby (Rock Hudson), the gardener.

When Sarah leaves, Carrie invites Ron to join her for lunch. While they are eating, Ron tells her that he intends to retire from the nursery business and raise trees.

Carrie's "children" arrive for the weekend. Ned is a student at Princeton and Kay is a social worker in New York. The children approve of Carrie's date. "I like Harvey," Kay says. "He's pleasant, amusing—*and* he acts his age. If there's anything I can't stand, it's an old goat. As Freud says, when we reach a certain age, sex becomes incongruous. I think Harvey understands that. All in all, he's remarkably civilized . . ."

Kay goes on to expound upon the way widows were treated in Egypt, protesting the fact that they were forced by the community to be interred with their dead husbands "along with all his other possessions." Then she adds airily, "Of course, that doesn't happen anymore."

"Doesn't it?" Carrie asks quietly. "Well, perhaps not in Egypt."

Ned is distressed by Carrie's low-cut red dress. He says he fears it will scare Harvey away. Kay accuses him of having an Oedipal reaction to his mother's sexual attractiveness. Harvey arrives and, over martinis, discusses the progress of his cold and the state of his liver.

At the club, Carrie is approached by a married masher named Howard. "You're beautiful, Carrie. Too beautiful to be lonely," he tells her, but she rebuffs him and he is repentant.

Back home later that evening, Harvey proposes marriage: "Of course I realize I'm not very romantic or impetuous. But then you'd hardly want that sort of thing. I'm sure you feel as I do. The companionship and the affection are the important things. I could give you those, Carrie." Carrie declines to give him a definite response.

Two weeks later, Ron reappears and finishes his work on Carrie's garden. He invites her to visit his home "out in the woods" where she can see the trees he is growing, particularly the silver-tip spruce. Carrie refuses and then reconsiders.

Carrie does not like Ron's cabin, but when they explore the old mill which belonged to Ron's grandfather, Carrie decides it would be a perfect place for him to settle down with some nice young girl. Ron tells her he's met plenty of girls, nice and otherwise, but none of them made him want to settle down. Then he delicately indicates his interest in Carrie, who acts discomfited.

"I'm sorry," she says. "I wasn't trying to arrange your life. After all, it's none of my business." A bird flies down from the rafters and frightens Carrie. She falls into Ron's arms and he kisses her.

In the next scene, Sarah invites Carrie to dinner at her house. "Look, Carrie, you can't sit around here with nothing to do." But Carrie is reluctant to attend because a vicious gossip named Mona will be present. Ron appears and invites Carrie to have dinner at the home of two of *his* friends. She accepts.

The friends, Mick and Aleta Anderson, live in a rustic, homey cabin in the country. Aleta introduces Carrie to the philosophical basis of their life-style, Thoreau's *Walden*. Carrie reads from it out loud:

> The mass of men lead lives of quiet desperation. Why should we be in such desperate haste to succeed? If a man does not keep pace with his companions, perhaps it is because he hears a different drummer. Let him step to the music he hears, however measured or far away.[5]

Ron never read *Walden,* Aleta tells Carrie. "He just lives it." She explains that Ron saved them from the pursuit of unimportant things, "keeping up with the Joneses," blindly pursuing security and financial success to the point that their marriage was endangered. "To thine own self be true—that's Ron," Aleta concludes.

Other people arrive, each contributing food for the dinner. They are a heterogeneous group in age and occupation: beekeepers, artists, birdwatchers—social dropouts who have elected an alternative lifestyle. Ron and Carrie sing and dance together and have a rousing, old-fashioned good time.

---

[5] Thoreau's message was considered such a threat to conformity that in 1954 the United States Information Service banned *Walden* from its libraries on the grounds that it was "downright socialistic." (Miller and Nowak, *The Fifties: The Way We Really Were* (Garden City, New York: Doubleday, 1977).

Afterward, Ron takes Carrie back to the old mill, which he has remodeled into a glamorous rustic retreat, and proposes to her. Distressed, Carrie breaks a Wedgwood teapot that Ron had painstakingly repaired for her and collapses in tears on the steps of the mill. Ron tenderly helps her on with her boots so that she can go home. But then they kiss and Carrie decides to spend the night.

Next morning when Ron and Carrie return to town, Mona the gossip spots them and contacts everyone, including Sarah. Sarah seeks Carrie out and voices the community protest and suspicions: he's a lowly gardener; she's an older woman with money; perhaps their affair preceded the death of Carrie's husband. But after admitting that she is a snob, Sarah invites Carrie to bring Ron to a cocktail party so the members of Carrie's set can get to know him.

On the night of the party, Carrie introduces Ron to her "children." Kay tells Ron that Carrie is "more conventional" than he may realize. "She has the innate desire for group approval, which most women have . . ." Ned is appalled that Carrie could consider replacing her husband, "a successful businessman, pillar of the community" with a man of Ron's stature. Shaken by these assaults, Carrie wants to drive to Sarah's party in *her* car rather than in Ron's wood-paneled station wagon, but Ron gently reminds her that such distinctions shouldn't matter.

The community awaits the couple's arrival like vultures. "So that's Carrie's nature boy," one of them comments. Howard is particularly abusive, since Carrie rebuffed him earlier. He accuses her of *pretending* to be a "perfect lady" and makes a pass at her. Ron assaults him, the community sides with "poor Howard," and Ron and Carrie leave.

Ned waits up for Carrie and tells her that Ron is "against everything that father stood for." He says he will be too ashamed to visit her after she is married. The next day Kay comes home hysterical, having overheard gossip that her mother was involved with Ron before her father died. Although she knows that isn't so, she admits that she cares what people think. "Do you love him so much you're willing to ruin all our lives?" she demands.

Subsequently, Carrie tells Ron that she wants to postpone the marriage and that she thinks they should live in *her* house when they eventually *do* marry. Ron says he cannot live that way, and he adds, "I won't let Ned nor Kay nor anyone else run our lives." Carrie says he is asking her to choose between him and her children and ends the relationship.

Sometime later, Carrie meets Ron by accident at a Christmas tree lot. They begin a reconciliation, but then Aleta's beautiful young cousin Mary Ann rushes over to Ron and accidentally gives the impression that she is involved with him. Carrie runs off, leaving Ron bewildered and twice rejected.

At Christmas, Kay announces she is engaged. Ned tells Carrie he is planning to go off to Paris and Iran as soon as he graduates, and recommends under the circumstances that they sell the house. The children's Christmas present to their mother is a television set, which Carrie earlier referred to as "the last refuge of the lonely woman." As Carrie stares forlornly at her reflection in the blank TV screen, the salesman intones its virtues: "Drama, comedy, life's parade at your fingertips."

Out hunting, Mick tells Ron that he should go to Carrie and prevail upon her to resume their relationship. Ron says he wants Carrie to make up her own mind. Mick leaves Ron to think things over.

Simultaneously, Carrie's physician, whom she has consulted about "miserable headaches," tells her to go after Ron. "What good was your noble sacrifice?" he demands. Carrie responds that Ron should have come to her. The doctor disagrees. "If you loved him, you'd have gone to him."

As Carrie leaves the doctor's office, she encounters Aleta, who tells her that Mary Ann has been engaged to a boy from New Jersey for the past year. Realizing she misunderstood Ron's relationship to Mary Ann, Carrie drives out to Ron's place. Ron sees her leaving as he is returning from hunting, but in his attempt to reach her before she drives off, he falls and is knocked unconscious.

Later that evening, Aleta appears at Carrie's home to report Ron's accident. Carrie returns with Aleta to the old mill and spends the night waiting for Ron to regain consciousness. She finally realizes what Ron stands for in "refusing to give importance to unimportant things. I let others make my decisions," she tells Aleta.

In the morning, Ron comes to and sees Carrie. She tells him, "Yes, darling, I've come home."

Perhaps the most striking element in the treatment of the story is the scant attention paid to the substantial age difference between Carrie and Ron. (This may result, in part, from the fact that the screenwriter, Peg Fenwick, was a woman.) Issues which might have been dwelled on, such as Carrie's jealous fantasies about Aleta's beautiful blonde cousin, and the fact that Ron and Carrie's son Ned *appear* to be the same age, are introduced merely to be discarded, as if to say that they aren't issues at all. Despite what Molly Haskell refers to as Carrie's "gentle, motherly concern" for Ron, she seems more often than not like a little girl.

Carrie was seventeen when she married Martin Scott and in many ways her development was arrested at that age. She was, as Betty Friedan describes in *The Feminine Mystique,* one of "those who choose the path of 'feminine adjustment'—evading . . . terror by marrying at eighteen, losing themselves in having babies and the details of housekeeping. . . . simply refusing to grow up, to face the question of their own identity."

Carrie's immaturity appears as a lack of authority in relation to her children, both of whom have a control over Carrie's behavior that she does not have over theirs. Kay repeatedly asserts her superiority to Carrie by virtue of her professional knowledge. Ned inherits his father's role as head of the household, serving the martinis, waiting up for Carrie after her date with Ron as if she is a teenager, deciding later that they should sell the house, and in general exercising sexual possessiveness of his mother, something Kay is quick to point out.

In addition, Carrie's emotional contemporaneity with her daughter is presented as a source of anxiety for Kay. Kay's speech about the inappropriateness of sex after a certain age is an attempt to relegate her mother to a "safe" middle age, where she is not a rival. For it becomes apparent that Carrie *is* a rival, competing with women who are Kay's age (like Mary Ann) and winning the love of a man who *appears* to be in the same age range as Kay's fiancé, Freddie (David Janssen).

Finally, Carrie and Ron oftentimes relate to one another as daughter and father. In their very first conversation, she asks him if she should take up gardening as an avocation, apparently assuming Ron has superior insight into what would make her life worthwhile. When Carrie is frightened by the sudden flight of a bird, she seeks protection in Ron's arms. Ron must remind her to wear a warm coat and help put on her boots; moreover, he is intermittently preoccupied with the possibility that she will catch cold. Ron acts as Carrie's mentor, reeducating her values (it shouldn't matter which car they take to Sarah's party) and urging her to be unafraid to make her own decisions. He is, in fact, the catalyst of Carrie's maturation, for, in order to be with him, she must achieve a modicum of independence from the secure but sterile world of her family and friends. However, the paternal limits placed on Carrie's growth are revealed when Carrie asks Ron, "You want me to be a man?" and Ron replies, "Only in that one way"—that is, only "man" enough to dare to marry him. (". . . thus men have been led, in their own interest, to give partial emancipation to women. . . ." Simone de Beauvoir wrote in *The Second Sex*.[6])

But in truth, what Ron wants of Carrie has nothing to do with manhood, and the film's inability to recognize that is part of what renders it reactionary and sexist rather than revolutionary. Ron confounds responsible politics, humane values, healthy sensuality, and a responsiveness to one's own needs with manhood. As Marlene Dixon writes in "The Rise of Women's Liberation," [7] "For those who believe in the 'rights of mankind,' 'the dignity of man,' consider that to make a woman a person, a human being in her own right, you would have to change her sex." Ironically, one element of the film's polemic is that the men who compose Carrie's milieu are *not* real human beings. Their lives are consumed by materialism;

---

[6] (New York: Alfred Knopf, 1952).
[7] *Masculine/Feminine: Readings in Sexual Mythology and the Liberation of Women*, ed. by Betty and Theodore Roszak (New York: Harper & Row, 1969).

their sexuality is immoral, perverse, or nonexistent; their relations with one another are savage and critical; their lives are lived in accordance with community standards, not in response to their individual desires.

In fact, the film does not intend to imply that men are exemplary. Rather, it contrasts dead men with living men (Martin Scott, the cold stone "pillar of the community" vs. Ron Kirby, the vibrant "silver-tip spruce") and dead women with living ones (Sarah vs. Aleta, their comparability established structurally by their roles as Carrie's confidantes and advisors, and visually by the fact that they both have red hair and resemble one another facially). But the movie falls into a semantic trap in its attempt to characterize *human* liberation because it is fundamentally opposed to *women's* liberation.

For example, the film treats Kay, the only "liberated" woman in the story, as a satirical caricature. She is portrayed as pompous and hypocritical, a mocker of male chauvinism but at the same time attracted to a male chauvinist "jock" who understands none of her intellectual ideas. "How can anyone so little be so smart?" Freddie asks. "And yet so pretty?" After he kisses her, she removes her glasses, as if to say that thinking and sexual responsiveness in a female are incompatible, and that a woman's intellect is a veneer that can be dropped as easily as glasses are removed. In fact, the film's devaluation of Kay only ceases when she tearfully confesses to her mother that she *does* care what people think, that she, in her own words, "has the innate desire for group approval, which most women have . . ." By deflating Kay's pretensions to being a superior woman by virtue of her intelligence, the film mitigates her power to symbolize an attractive alternative for Carrie or the women in the audience.

Aleta, not Kay, is the film's female role model. She is an exemplary eighteenth-century American wife, "defined not in terms of herself, but in terms of her relation to men: Adam's rib, Adam's temptress, Adam's helpmate, Adam's wife and mother of his children." [8] While

---

[8] David C. McClelland, "Wanted: A New Self-Image for Women," *The Woman in America*, ed. Robert J. Lifton (Boston: Beacon Press, 1967).

Aleta has both dignity and the appearance of autonomy, her satellite identity is affirmed by a subtle subservience to men and the limitation of her functions to those consistent with women's traditional role. For example, Aleta makes reference to *Walden* as "Mick's bible," and speaks reverently of Ron as someone who follows Thoreau's dictates instinctively, but she fails to mention her own commitment and contribution to, and her thorough understanding of, their anti-establishment life-style. Another subtle illustration of Aleta's subordination occurs when she obediently responds to her husband's reminder that she had "better get busy" with the preparations for the dinner before the other guests arrive.

These hints of an inequality in status are confirmed when Mick tells Ron during their hunting expedition that Carrie "doesn't want to make up her own mind. No girl does. She wants you to make it up *for* her." The film, however, definitively rejects Mick's arrogant dismissal of women's ability to make their own decisions, and thereby postulates for Ron and Carrie an even more ideal alliance.

In support of this ideal, Ron's remodeling of the old mill is a symbolic gesture toward widening his male ethic to accommodate a woman like Carrie. It is a compromise in the direction of material comfort which Ron makes out of love for Carrie and respect for her needs. Ron's flexibility and his willingness to share Carrie's values insofar as he can without compromising his integrity are also expressed when he accompanies Carrie to Sarah's party and when he repairs the Wedgwood teapot Carrie found abandoned in the old mill. This is, unarguably, a good man, who will give Carrie a good life. But that is precisely the problem. As long as men *give* women their lives, women are dependent, and therefore not free.

The need to maintain women's dependence arises from men's dependence on women (beginning with the basic biological fact that women, in giving birth to men and providing their nourishment, give men *their* lives). This dependence is suggested by Ron's nearly fatal accident when he pursues Carrie, and his helplessness on the sofa where he lies between life and death. Revelations of male vulnerability are a staple of the fifties, so much so that one tends to grow suspicious of them, not necessarily because they aren't true but because they are wielded so manipulatively. Just as women in their dependency on men became skilled in the art of "soft, persuasive and somewhat devious" manipulative domination, a "method of indirection" based on hurt which they tried "ever so hard to conceal,"[9] so men appeared in the fifties to be *using* their helplessness as a device to hold onto women.

Adam's Rib (1949) makes this phenomenon comically explicit when Spencer Tracy feigns despondency and tears to regain Katharine Hepburn's love, demonstrating that he can use a "woman's trick" just as well as she can. And it is implicit when Ron, after regaining consciousness at the end of *All That Heaven Allows,* says, "Carrie, you've come home." On the one hand, "home is where the heart is"; on the other, home is also "woman's place."

Carrie, a woman in transition from an old life to a new one, is liberated from the clutches of a moribund middle-class community into the arms of a loving leftist-radical man. But, as Robin Morgan wrote in 1970, "How much further we will have to go to create those profound changes that would give birth to a genderless society. . . . *Beyond all known standards,* especially those easily articulated revolutionary ones we all rhetorically invoke."[10]

---

[9] Edward Strecker, *Their Mother's Sons* (1946). Quoted in Betty Friedan's *The Feminine Mystique* (New York: Dell, 1963).
[10] "Goodbye to All That," *Masculine/Feminine: Readings in Sexual Mythology and the Liberation of Women,* ed. by Betty and Theodore Roszak (New York: Harper & Row, 1969).

10

A Minimal Feast

Picnic (1956)

Live, live, live! Life is a banquet and most of you poor suckers are starving to death.

Rosalind Russell, Auntie Mame (1959)

Anna Karenina, describing her feelings about her lover Count Vronsky in the recent BBC production of Tolstoy's novel, says, "I feel like a starving man when someone gives him food." But Anna's fatal plunge beneath the wheels of a speeding train suggests that emotional starvation leads to tragedy more often than it leads to fulfillment. For the obsessive character of starvation breeds a desperation which precludes rational judgment. Hollywood, however, has consistently *availed* itself of the American public's irrationality by feeding its starvation for easy solutions with wish-fulfilling fictions about emotionally hungry women. Not merely have happy endings been imposed where unhappy ones would have been more appropriate. Fantasy happiness has been applied like a Band-Aid to prevent the audience from perceiving a need for *real change* in women's lives. For, if female happiness can be achieved in a movie *despite the way things are,* then change is not necessary.

Love and marriage have been a traditional means for women to attain happiness in Hollywood movies, but films of the fifties "enriched" this formulaic resolution with the introduction of sexual passion. In *Picnic* (as in *From Here to Eternity*), the ultimate in human desire is represented by an instance of choreographed eroticism: in the film's most celebrated scene, Kim Novak glides toward William Holden in a rhythmic trance to the hit tune "Moonglow" and they perform a ritualistic Midwestern mating dance while the other members of the cast watch with jealous fascination. So tantalizing is this depiction of perfect passion that the disturbing *reality* which surrounds it sheds the impact it would have in real life and becomes peripheral. As Michael Wood explains in *America in the Movies,* "[popular films] permit us to look without looking at things we can neither face fully nor entirely disavow. We don't usually notice this function, but then it is because we don't notice—because the distress lurking in *Picnic* . . . merely lurks and never pounces—that these movies work so well as myths."

But what is the distress in *Picnic* that we could "neither face fully nor entirely disavow"? It appears to be nothing less than the conviction that life for all but the lucky few (men as well as women) is a bust.

Arthur Miller is the most eloquent spokesman of this middle-class, peculiarly fifties lament. But certainly second is William Inge, who wrote *Come Back, Little Sheba* and *The Dark at the Top of the Stairs* as well as *Picnic*. These are, for the most part, little-life dramas of men and women who never caught the brass rings and in the process of trying lost the only thing they had—youth. As Michael Wood summarizes, "In fifties films people kept asking where *everything* went wrong . . ."

But no one, least of all the middle-brow writers of the fifties, appeared to suspect that the social or psychic anorexia they were experiencing was, at least in part, the product of their own impoverished bourgeois values and exhausted style of life. Rather, they perceived the condition of the fifties in permanent terms, and the immediate limitations of life at that time (particularly for women) as permanent limitations—something Henrik Ibsen, for example, did *not* do in his dramas of women's psychic claustrophobia, *A Doll's House* and *Hedda Gabler*.

This American misapprehension of social and human reality as an unchangeably grim absolute fostered the need for some compensatory solace, which Inge provided in the erotic attraction of his two protagonists. Of course, Inge—a realist—took no pains to hide that his sexual solution was largely expedient: Novak's mother, the victim of a passionate romance which foundered in marriage, tells Novak precisely how her life with Holden will turn out. But since the movie provides no *other* choices, nor even an awareness of the possibility that other choices might exist, both the characters and the audience are forced back upon sex as the sole salvation in life and are encouraged to blissfully anticipate the prospect of sharing a basement room in a Tulsa hotel with a good-looking bellhop.

The movie begins with a shot of a freight train arriving in a Midwestern town on Labor Day. Hal Carter (William Holden) emerges from one of the cars like a hobo. He wanders over to the houses which border the tracks and offers to do odd jobs for an old lady named Mrs. Helen Potts (Verna Felton) in exchange for breakfast. As he is working, bare-chested, he attracts the attention of the women who live next door. Rosemary Sydney (Rosalind Russell), an "old-maid schoolteacher," is first fascinated, then embarrassed to be seen in curlers and cold cream, and finally indignant. "Workin' over there naked as an Indian!" she tells Millie (Susan Strasberg), the tomboy-intellectual younger daughter of the woman with whom she boards. Millie attempts to get an optimal view but is interrupted by the arrival of Bomber (Nick Adams), the newspaper delivery boy, who calls Millie "goonface" and makes a play for Millie's beautiful older sister Madge (Kim Novak). Hal intervenes on Madge's behalf and Bomber demands to know who he is. "What's that matter?" Hal asks coolly. "I'm bigger than you are." He bounces a basketball off Bomber's forehead to punctuate his assertion of superiority.

Flo Owens (Betty Field), the mother of the two girls, emerges from her house and reacts to Hal with immediate antagonism. "Is there something you want, young man?" she asks him coldly. "Just loafin'," Hal replies, no match for this woman. "Well, this is a busy day for us," Flo snaps. "We have no time to loaf."

Hal goes off to visit Alan Benson (Cliff Robertson), a former fraternity brother and the son of a wealthy grain elevator owner. Hal recounts to Alan his activities since college: gas station attendant, soldier, aspiring movie star, and ranch hand.

The film cuts back to Madge and her mother. Flo urges Madge to "get busy" landing Alan Benson. "If a girl loses her chance when she's young, she might as well throw all her prettiness away." Madge protests that she's only nineteen. Flo retorts that next year she'll be twenty, then forty.

Millie and Madge get into a jealous squabble. "Madge is the pretty one," Millie chants, and then attacks her for being "so dumb they almost had to burn the schoolhouse down to get her out of it." She points out that all Madge can do is "work in a dimestore." Madge, echoing Bomber, calls Millie a "goonface." Millie runs off in tears.

"Poor Millie," Flo says, and Madge replies, "Poor Millie won herself a scholarship for four whole years of college." "A girl like Millie can need confidence in other ways," Flo insists, discounting her younger daughter's intellectual accomplishments. Then she goes on to portray the advantages in Madge's marrying Alan: comfort, charge accounts in all the stores, automobiles, trips, the country club, all available to Madge because she is pretty. "What good is it just to be pretty?" Madge demands, and says she gets tired of merely being looked at. She wonders if Flo loves Millie more than her.

A similar rivalry exists between Hal and Alan. Hal envies Alan's intellect, his academic achievements (Hal attended college on a football scholarship and was slated to be an All American before he flunked out), and his wealthy father. He tells Alan that his own father, an alcoholic, was scraped off the pavement and died in jail. Hal asks Alan for a job, but his fantasy is to be an executive with a desk, secretaries, and a phone. "I know I gotta get someplace in this world. I just gotta." Alan cautions Hal to be patient and invites him along on the Labor Day picnic.

The picnic begins innocently with local talent, three-legged races, pie-eating contests, and treasure hunting in a haystack. But as the afternoon fades, desperation begins to emerge. Hal brags about the boots his father left him and lies to give his father some worldly importance. Flo and Helen Potts, surrounded by young lovers, reminisce about their lost youth and the disappointments they have endured: Flo's husband abandoned her with two young daughters, and Helen Potts's life has been devoted to caring for her invalid mother. As the sun sets, Rosemary, the schoolteacher, remarks to her boyfriend Howard Bevins (Arthur O'Connell), "It's like the daytime didn't want to end, isn't it? It's like the daytime's going to put up a big scrap, set the world on fire, to keep the night from creeping on."

A little later, Alan, preoccupied with his father's disapproval of Madge, who literally lives on the other side of the tracks, tells her that Benson will be won over when she becomes queen of Nee-wollah (Halloween spelled backwards) that evening. "He's always impressed by people who win things, or make the most money, or score the most points at a football game," Alan explains, unwittingly revealing his jealousy of Hal as an athlete.

In the next scene, spectators gather at the river and chant "Nee-wollah" as Madge, resplendent in red velvet and roses, emerges from the darkness into the spotlight in a canoe, like Cleopatra on her barge. Rosemary, watching from the sidelines, insists she was just as good-looking as Madge when she was a girl. Howard confesses to Hal that he is attracted to Madge but knows he "couldn't touch her with a ten-foot pole."

Hal tries to dance with Millie, but Millie can't follow the steps. Madge slowly moves onto the dance floor, doing the steps perfectly, and begins to dance with Hal. Rosemary suddenly assaults Hal, demanding to see his legs and then insisting he dance with her. "Ride 'em, cowboy," she cries, and recalls another cowboy who liked her because she was an older woman "and had some sense." She tells Hal he reminds her of statues of Roman gladiators. When he pulls away from her to return to Madge, she clings to his shirt so desperately that the shirt tears.

Howard cautions her to let the "young people" alone. "Young!

What do you mean, they're young!" Rosemary explodes. Millie becomes ill, the combined result of jealousy and alcohol. When Flo demands to know who permitted Millie to get drunk, Rosemary vindictively points the finger at Hal:

> Millie was your date; you should have been looking after her. But you were too busy making eyes at Madge. . . . You've been stomping around here in those boots like you owned the place, thinkin' every woman you saw was gonna fall madly in love. Well, here's one woman didn't pay you any mind. Bragging about your father! Bet he wasn't any better than you are. Strutting around here like some putty Apollo. You think just because you act young, you can walk in here and make off with whatever you like. Let me tell you something—you're a fake. You're no jive kid, you're just scared to act your age. Find yourself a mirror sometime and take a look in it. It won't be many years now before you'll be counting the gray hairs, if you're got any left. What'll happen to you then? You'll end your life in the gutter, and it'll serve you right. Because the gutter's where you came from and the gutter's where you belong.

Like a witch's curse, Rosemary's diatribe freezes everyone. Alan enters the scene, surveys the situation, and decides Hal is responsible for what has happened. "Same old Hal," he says bitterly. Hal runs off and Madge follows him.

Rosemary is stunned by her own outburst. She rationalizes to Howard that she merely wanted to have a good time on the last day of summer vacation. Howard asks her to come for a ride. She agrees, crying out desperately, "I want to have a good time."

Off by themselves, Madge reassures Hal that he's "young" and "witty" and "a wonderful dancer." When Hal insists that Rosemary was right about his being "a bum," Madge kisses him and they presumably make love.

In a parallel scene, Rosemary asks Howard to rescue her from her desolate life:

> It's no good living like this. Rented rooms, meeting a bunch of old ladies for supper every night. Coming back home alone.

> Each year I keep telling myself it's the last. Something will happen. Nothing ever does. Except I get a little crazier all the time.

She alludes to the fact that she has permitted Howard to make love to her for the first time, and begs him to marry her, asking that he come for her in the morning. Howard makes no promises.

Hal returns the car Alan lent him for the picnic and encounters the police, to whom Alan reported his car stolen. Hal says it is Madge, not the car, that Alan feels robbed of and escapes from the police, this time stealing Benson's car in earnest.

He seeks refuge with Howard Bevins, who forlornly contemplates the prospect of marrying Rosemary. The next morning, Howard brings Hal to see Madge. Rosemary misunderstands Howard's presence. "Girls, girls, here's my man!" she cries, announcing their imminent marriage to the teachers who've come by to pick her up for the first day of school. Howard dazedly acquiesces. They leave for a honeymoon in the Ozarks.

Hal tells Madge he's going to take a job as a bellhop in another town and asks her to join him there so that they can be married. He runs off to hop a freight, leaving as he arrived.

Flo frantically attempts to dissuade Madge from following Hal. "He's no good," she cries. "He'll never be able to support you. And when he *does* have a job, he'll spend it on drink. And after that, there'll be other women. I *know*."

"Mom," Madge replies unflappably, "you don't love someone because he's perfect." She breaks away from Flo's grip and proudly boards a bus, waving to Millie, who is on her way to school.

In a final aerial shot, with music soaring optimistically on the soundtrack, we see the bus in hot pursuit of the train.

John Gassner, in *Best American Plays: Fourth Series 1951–1957*,[1] is troubled by *Picnic*'s "happy" ending as a Broadway *play*. Calling it a "somewhat facile" resolution to a work which captured " 'something of the mischance and misbegottenness of life itself,' " he goes on to describe the circumstances surrounding its existence:

---

[1] (New York: Crown Publishers, 1958).

The director, Mr. Joshua Logan [who also directed the film], had sought an "upbeat" resolution for a "downbeat" play, and the author had complied with the request for an optimistic conclusion. The rewards in box-office terms were unmistakable, but the question remained whether the original conclusion, in which the heroine does not follow her lover, should have been sacrificed.

But while the play's ending generates a superficial sense of optimism, it is balanced by Inge's ironic qualifications and subtleties of characterization, which call the optimism into doubt.

For example, in the *play* Madge has a dream of a life other than marriage:

I always wonder, maybe some wonderful person is getting off here, just by accident, and he'll come into the dimestore for something and see me behind the counter, and he'll study me very strangely and then decide I'm just the person they're looking for in Washington for an important job in the Espionage Department. (*She is carried away.*) Or maybe he wants me for some great medical experiment that'll save the whole human race.

Even after Hal arrives, Madge continues to wait for someone *else* to come along, and the first act ends with Madge listening to a train whistle in the distance. The irony of the play is that Hal is *all* life delivers for Madge.

The movie, on the other hand, gives Madge no dream whatsoever. It thereby makes marriage to Alan or Hal Madge's only option, and then discredits Alan as a materialistic choice and something less than a "real man," giving Hal the edge by virtue of his honest poverty and masculine charisma. The movie even goes so far as to falsify Millie's character and wrench logic to confirm Madge's choice of Hal. When Madge vacillates about following Hal to Tulsa, Millie says:

When I graduate from college, I'm going to New York and write novels that'll shock people right out of their senses. I'm never going to fall in love—not me. I'm not going to live in some jerkwater town, and marry some ornery guy and raise

a lot of grimy kids. But just because *I'm* a dope doesn't mean
you have to be . . . Go with him, Madge. For once in your
life, do something bright.

The sudden turn-about, in which Millie refers to herself as a dope
for wanting to lead an independent life and urges Madge to do the
"bright" thing by surrendering herself to a dreary domestic existence, is not in the Broadway play, for the play merely sought an
"upbeat" ending. The film's ending, in contrast, is a concession to
the cultural imperative of the fifties to poison the well of women's
choices by making even the most dreadful marriage seem divine in
comparison to a solitary life.

A comparable worship of domesticity arose during the nineteenth
century in reaction against the movement for women's suffrage. As
Kathryn Weibel observes in *Mirror Mirror: Images of Women Reflected in Popular Culture* (1977),[2] "in an ironic sort of way, the
status of independent women in the real world was slowly being
advanced at the same time that the image of the passive, marriage-
oriented heroine was proliferating." But it wasn't ironic at all! This
reactionary counterforce, in both the nineteenth century and in
the fifties, was merely evidence of the threat that women's emancipation posed to the collective imagination of the culture during
these transitional times, and perhaps the best evidence that the
emancipation was gaining ground.

Millie is the personification of that threat. Although she is pretty
enough for all practical purposes, she is perceived as disabled by the
other characters in the story because she is also intelligent, creative,
and athletic. Hal refers to her in the film as "some sort of genius"
and as such she holds no attraction for him. Madge, on the other
hand, makes *him* "feel important." That is her talent and the only
one which counts for a woman in the world of the film.

In the *play*, however, Inge depicts Millie—and Rosemary, her
adult counterpart—not as victims of their gifts and abilities but of
a civilization which will not permit them to be both lovers and intelligent, independent human beings. He makes a strong thematic

---

[2] (New York: Anchor Press).

Picnic. The brainy tomboy Millie (Susan Strasberg) and her pretty but dumb sister Madge (Kim Novak) trade insults, while their mother Flo (Betty Field) helps make Madge a dream girl who can barter her beauty for a better life. Madge's flouncy domination of the space reflects her status as the ideal woman in the film. Millie, off to one side, bears the clichéd emblems of her type: glasses, a book, braids, and boyish clothing.

point of the degrading capitulation women must make to men in order to be loved. Flo, "a little bitterly," answers Madge's inquiry whether she loved her husband by saying, "Some women are humiliated to love a man. . . . Because—a woman is weak to begin with, I suppose, and sometimes—her love for him makes her feel— almost helpless. And maybe she fights him—'cause her love makes her seem so dependent."

This struggle between love and autonomy is the basis of Inge's female characterizations in the play. Rosemary Sydney repeatedly asserts her pride in being independent. When Mrs. Potts comments that "you schoolteachers do have nice things," Rosemary re-

Picnic. The ideal and the real are contrasted in this mating dance sequence. As Madge and Hal (William Holden) move blissfully in the foreground, Rosemary (Rosalind Russell) drunkenly denigrates the bony legs of her boyfriend Howard (Arthur O'Connell). Each wishes to trade places with the ideal couple.

torts, "And don't have to ask anybody when we wanta get 'em, either." In a stage direction, Inge writes that Rosemary's "tone of voice must tell a man she is independent of him," and later that both Millie and Rosemary "seem to show a little arrogance in dancing together, as though boasting to the men of their independence." Later, Rosemary attacks Hal for exercising his male prerogative: "You think just 'cause you're a man, you can walk in here and make off with whatever you like. . . . You think just 'cause you're strong you can show your muscles and nobody'll know what a pitiful specimen you are." Thus, when Rosemary finally "sinks to her knees," "weeps pathetic tears," and—"beaten and humble"—beseeches Howard to marry her, there is a measure of defeat in the play, the triumph of one human need at the expense of another.

The same struggle and defeat are prophesied for Millie in the play. When Hal asks Millie to dance, she responds, "Well I never danced with boys. I always have to lead." Hal tells her, "Now look, kid, you gotta remember *I'm* the *man,* and you gotta do the steps *I* do." Millie replies, "I keep wantin' to do the steps I make up myself," and Hal responds, "The man's gotta take the lead, kid, as long as he's able." Unable to accept this, Millie eventually protests that she's "never gonna fall in love." But Mrs. Potts cautions her to "Wait till you're a little older before you say that, Millie-girl."

Even Madge, though far less conflicted than Rosemary and Millie, is shown in the play to resist the fall into love. In a stage direction, "Madge utters [Hal's] name in a voice of resignation" before she goes off to make love with him, and later she asks her mother "in a wail of anguish,"

> Oh, Mom, what can you do with the love you feel? Where is there you can take it?

These capitulations to love and marriage are presented in the play as a sacrifice of self-determination, a bargain women feel forced to strike with life. Inge's only failure is that he represents this compromise as an inevitability of women's existence, rather than a result of women's restrictive social role.

The film, in contrast, eliminates or changes most of the basis of the women's internal conflict. Madge's anguish is made to seem like a reaction to growing up and leaving home, a *fear* of self-direction rather than a fear of its *loss*. Millie and Rosemary's independence is portrayed as nothing more than a prideful cover-up of their desperate desire to be loved and their fear of rejection because they are not as attractive to men as Madge. Millie's beautifully succinct admission in the play that she can't help wanting to do her *own* dance steps is dropped, along with Hal's insistence that *he* must lead. And virtually none of Rosemary's resentment of Hal's male prerogative, his *right* to "take the lead" and expect that women follow, is preserved. Instead, her diatribe is reduced to a dramatization of "hell hath no fury like a woman scorned" and its content is altered to an attack on Hal's *youth,* emphasizing her jealousy of youth and her terror of growing old alone, which she projects onto him. "It won't be many years now before you'll be counting the gray hairs . . . What'll happen to you then?" This shift from understandably savage resentment in the play to neurotically savage desperation in the film changes Rosemary from a conflicted woman who's not sure she *wants* to love a man, to a caricaturish love-starved spinster who can't get a man to love *her.*

The film also eliminates *Flo's* resentment of female dependence. Her revelation of her feelings toward her husband, and her line to Madge that "Alan is the kind of man who doesn't mind if a woman's bossy," are both deleted. As a result, it is impossible to perceive Flo as the *source* of Millie's independence, or to understand *why* the more dependent Madge suspects Flo loves Millie more than her. In addition, the omission of this crucial aspect of Flo's psychology makes her obsession with Madge marrying Alan seem purely *materialistic,* rather than a misguided attempt to barter Madge's beauty for the independence that a practical (as opposed to a romantic) marriage would provide.

This change is meant to discredit Flo. Even though the movie makes it clear (even clearer than the play) that Flo has good reason—the experience of her own life—to be an enemy of romance, it also asserts that any alternatives to romance are infinitely worse.

In this way, the film makes room for Hal's considerable deficiencies—his desperate lies and foolish dreams of grandeur and superficial bravado—without endangering his position as the romantic hero. In fact, it makes enough room to accommodate a hero whose vulnerability, beneath all those rippling muscles, is the basis of his appeal.

This first becomes clear when Hal tells Alan about two tough women who forced him to make love to them at gunpoint ("Gee, they must have thought I was Superman.") and then robbed him of all his money. "I'm telling you, Benson, women are getting desperate," Hal concludes, but his story suggests, rather, that women are getting stronger while he grows weaker.

Hal is portrayed as an endangered species, as anachronistic as the hairy mammoth or the caveman. "There's no place in the world for a guy like me," he tells Madge after Rosemary has lit into him. "Women like Miss Sydney make me mad at the whole female sex," Madge replies.

The film would have the audience believe that "women like Miss Sydney" and the two gunslingers are destroying "real men," and that only women like Madge can save them. As Hal tells Madge:

> Listen, baby, you're the only *real* thing I ever wanted, ever. You're mine. I've got to claim what's mine or I'll be nothing as long as I live.

Hal needs Madge so absolutely that she has the power by virtue of her love to make him "something," whereas otherwise he is "nothing." After Rosemary's verbal assault, it becomes Madge's mission in life to restore and sustain Hal's crumbling manhood; and making him "something" makes her "something" in turn. That is the symbiotic nature of "real manhood" and "real womanhood" which the film doggedly celebrates.

Mrs. Potts is the sweet-tempered champion of these traditional roles in the film:

> I got so used to things as they were. Everything so prim. The geranium in the window. And then *he* walked in. And it was different. He clomped through the place like he was still outdoors. There was a man in the house. And it seemed good.

Mrs. Potts, like Madge, continually comes to Hal's rescue, feeding him, admiring him, defending him, and supporting him, and at one point Hal refers to her as his "best girl." As the play suggests, Mrs. Potts "intuitively . . . says what is needed to save his ego." But the *play* also makes it clear that womanhood is a sort of enslavement. Just as Mrs. Potts is tied to her mother, Madge is tied to the kitchen when Millie goes off to swim with Hal and Alan.

> *Hal:* Isn't your sister goin' with us?
> *Millie:* Madge has to cook lunch.
> *Hal:* Do you mean *she cooks?*
> *Millie:* Sure! Madge cooks and sews and does all those things that women do.

Millie, less of a "woman," is shown in the *play* to be more free than Madge as a human being. But this point is lost in the film, when Madge goes swimming along with Millie. For the film does not want women's sacrifice to *seem* like a sacrifice.

Nonetheless, the film's subliminal message is that it takes *two* people to make a "real man," the man himself and the woman who sacrifices herself to his welfare. And since it is the film's burden to promote that sacrifice, it represents abnegation as the only positive option for women, the only act which affirms their womanhood, and the only source of their most coveted satisfactions: sexual passion and the man's enthralled dependency. As a recent ad for a romance pulp novel in *Good Housekeeping* magazine expresses it:

> Cyra's emerald eyes and flaming hair brought 30,000 pieces of gold at auction—more than her father, Lord Glenkirk of Scotland, could raise for her ransom. For young Lady Janet Leslie there would be no escaping the harem of Sultan Selim. But from the first moment their souls touched, the Sultan was lost to her forever—to his beautiful Cyra, "the flame." She belonged to him completely—yet it was he who felt enslaved.[3]

This garbage of solace, excitement, and lies fed to women, and fed upon by women, to justify and help them endure their drab little lives functions precisely like the "picnic." As Mrs. Potts tells Flo in the *play*:

> I think we plan picnics just to give ourselves an excuse—to let something thrilling happen in our lives.

The sexism of the fifties (like the "Total Woman" movement of the seventies), in its assertion of a slavish domesticity, drained life of vitality, surprise, and options, except insofar as sex could be stretched to suffice for all of these. In other words, the fifties created and defended its own psychic starvation.

But the implosion of the fifties also generated an explosive opposition which certain films of the decade recorded. *Auntie Mame* (1959), celebrating an iconoclastic woman who abhorred the empti-

---

[3] An ad for Bertrice Small's *The Kadin,* an Avon Paperback, February, 1978.

ness and impoverishment of middle-class values and scorned the traditional female role except as an occasional comic romp, was one. In its appearance at the end of the decade, it constituted an assault upon the "little lives" of mid-century America. *Auntie Mame* was a declaration of political and social revolt against human—and specifically female—oppression, the "mind-forged manacles" that reduced life's banquet to a picnic.

11

Brides of Christ

Heaven Knows, Mr. Allyson (1957) and The Nun's Story (1958)

The perfect nun is one who, for the love of God, is obedient in all things unto death. . . . you are only an instrument. In yourself you are nothing. . . . Each sister shall understand that on entering the convent, she has made the sacrifice of her life to God.

Instructions to postulants in The Nun's Story

The ideal wife is one who does everything that the ideal husband likes, and nothing else. Now to treat a person as a means instead of an end is to deny that person's right to live. . . . woman, if she dares face the fact that she is being so treated, must either loathe herself or else rebel.

George Bernard Shaw, The Quintessence of Ibsenism *(1891)*

T he appearance in the fifties of two major films about nuns is not, in itself, extraordinary. American audiences over the decades have delighted in the depiction of worldly nuns, women who, like Ingrid Bergman in *The Bells of St. Mary's* (1945), revealed themselves to be "regular guys" who laughed and ran, played baseball and boxed, and "knew the score." But never before the fifties did films about nuns assert their professional equality with secular men or suggest that obedience to even the most exalted Male Authority might no longer be endurable, or even necessary.

The paradoxical status of the nun as a lifetime professional career-woman symbolically married to God rendered her an ideal persona in the fifties through which to express the reality of women's emancipation without revealing it to be emancipation or permitting it to constitute a threat to conventional secular life-styles. For, while the nun is a professional female role model, and her existence as part of a women's religious community renders her an exemplar of sisterhood and female bonding, her professional activities (as educator, healer, caregiver, missionary) are a measure of her service to God. Her work is subject to, and validated by, her Heavenly Husband; therefore, it did not challenge male supremacy or the female domestic imperative of the fifties.

John Huston's *Heaven Knows, Mr. Allyson* makes use of the nun's contradictory status to dilute and disguise the liberated plot formula of his classic film *The African Queen* (1950). In both movies, a man and a woman of opposite sensibilities, thrust together in an isolated location by the circumstances of war, collaborate to outwit the Enemy and simultaneously grow to love one another. But *Heaven Knows, Mr. Allyson,* made in the thick of the fifties' escalating repression of women, does not maintain the sexual equality of the earlier film.

In *The African Queen*, Rose (Katharine Hepburn) contributes as much as Charley (Humphrey Bogart) to their survival, navigating the African Queen through hazardous rapids, suggesting a way to repair the boat's propeller when it cracks, and eventually joining Charley in a leech-filled swamp to pull the boat toward open water. More-over, it is *Rose's* idea to sabotage a German ship and *her* plan to destroy it with makeshift torpedoes.

Sister Angela (Deborah Kerr), the nun in *Heaven Knows, Mr. Allyson,* initially shares some of her prototype's independent spirit. When her accidental companion on a deserted Pacific island, a Marine named Mr. Allyson (Robert Mitchum), is pulled from his raft by a turtle he's attempting to catch for dinner, Sister Angela recovers both him and the turtle from the water. In addition, she is game to attempt a 300-mile raft ride to Fiji. But when Japanese soldiers occupy the island and the couple are forced to hide in a cave, Mr. Allyson takes over in the traditional male manner, feeding and protecting Sister Angela. And it is he who devises a plan to aid an Allied invasion of the island, although he credits Sister Angela with inspiring him to seek God's guidance (hence the title of the film) and, in a gently comic moment, appears to receive the idea from God.

Since Sister Angela, as a good nun, *cannot* contribute directly to the destruction of the Enemy, it is understandable why Allyson is made responsible for devising the sabotage. But the other changes in the film, which turn Allyson into shining knight and Sister Angela into helpless maiden, are a product of the fifties' campaign to reestablish the power imbalance of the traditional sexual roles.

Nonetheless, under the cover of this concession to the prevailing spirit of the times, the film asserts the professional equality of its protagonists, which becomes the basis of their abiding friendship. Mr. Allyson tells Sister Angela, "A Marine. That's what I am. All through me. A Marine! Like you're a nun. You've got your cross. I've got my globe and anchor. . . ." Allyson describes the drill instructor who was responsible for transforming him into a Marine and concludes, "Other guys, you know, most of them—they got homes, families. Me, I got the Corps, like you got the Church." Sister Angela agrees that the Marines and the Convent "have many things in common. . . . You should have known *my* D.I., Sister Brigida, the mistress of novices. They had a name for her, too. We called her the —the Holy Terror." When Allyson confesses that he can't understand why beautiful women would want to be nuns, Sister Angela replies tartly, "Well, maybe there are some as wouldn't understand a man wanting to be a Marine." Sometime later, Allyson cautions Sister Angela not to be disturbed when he rises at five-thirty in the morning; she responds that it is her custom as a nun to rise at five. "Sounds like you're in a pretty tough outfit, ma'am," Allyson concedes. "It 'tis, Mr. Allyson. It 'tis."

The African Queen. Rosie (Katharine Hepburn) joins Charley (Humphrey Bogart) in a leech-filled swamp. Theirs is a relationship of complete equality, in which the tasks of survival are shared.

Heaven Knows, Mr. Allyson. The balance of power shifts to the man (Robert Mitchum) in this reworking of the *African Queen* narrative formula. Sister Angela (Deborah Kerr) crouches down apprehensively as Mr. Allyson stands ready to defend their lives with a knife.

It is safe to say that a nun's career was the only unassailable female profession in the fifties. No one could argue that she should quit her job and get married, because she was *already* married—to Christ—and quitting would mean, according to Sister Angela, the loss of her "immortal soul." No one would be threatened by the assertion of her equality with a Marine because, more than anything else, it was an equality of subservience to a higher male authority. And finally, no one would perceive a nun as a revolutionary woman because nuns were nothing new. Their existence, their appearance, their practices were all firmly rooted in the past. That is why John Huston used a nun as the harbinger of America's emerging feminism.

But if Sister Angela was the harbinger of new womanhood, the nun in Fred Zinnemann's *The Nun's Story* was new womanhood itself. In this film, a nun uses marriage to Christ as a way to evade secular marriage and thereby safeguard her career as a nurse, only to discover that Christ as the Ultimate Husband is the Absolute Enemy

of female career aspirations. *The Nun's Story*'s emphasis on the
marriage metaphor (which plays no part in Kathryn Hulme's novel
from which the film was adapted), and its dramatization of the
conflict between the "wife's" professional dedication and the "husband's" marital demands, renders it an unwitting [1] allegory of the
demise of conventional secular marriage and the age-old female conflict between service to the self and surrender of the self to the male
other.

The Nun's Story begins in Belgium on the day in 1929 when
Gabrielle Van der Mal (Audrey Hepburn) leaves home to become a
nun. We see her put a note and an engagement ring beside a heart-
shaped photograph of a man named Jean whom we never meet.

---

[1] When Zinnemann visited Yale in 1977, I asked him about the secular implications of his film. He said he did not consciously attempt to draw a secular
parallel; but he was receptive to the idea that *The Nun's Story* anticipated
female rebellion against the supremacy of the male within countless secular
marriages in subsequent decades.

As Gabrielle and her father, the eminent surgeon Dr. Hubert Van der Mal (Dean Jagger), walk to the convent, he says, "Gaby, I can see you poor, I can see you chaste, but I cannot see you, a strong-willed girl, obedient to those bells." Gaby replies, "In the Congo, Father, they'll be calling me to work I love."

At the convent, Sister Marguerite (Mildred Dunnock), mistress of postulants and "a Living Rule" (i.e., a perfect nun), takes Gaby's dowry from Dr. Van der Mal. By way of parting, Gaby says, "I'll do my best. I want you to be proud of me." Her father replies, "I don't want to be proud of you. I want you to be happy." A door closes sharply between the outside world and the inner sanctum of the convent.

A lengthy period of instruction ensues, governed by Sister Marguerite and the Reverend Mother Emmanuel (Dame Edith Evans), who "represents Christ among us and as such . . . is loved and obeyed by us." Sister Marguerite teaches the rule of silence, "exterior and interior silence" to permit "constant conversation with God," and obedience to the bells, "the voice of God." Mother Emmanuel preaches humility and sacrifice:

> The sacrifices that are required of us are bearable only if we make them with love. Just as in the world we can do impossible things with a glad heart for a loved one, so it is with us. We can endure greater sacrifice because the object of our love is our Lord Jesus Christ.

Mother Emmanuel speaks of "exercises in humility, these steps toward a closer union with our crucified Lord" as something which one must accept or "you do not belong with us." She reminds the postulants that "cloistered life is made up of an infinity of small things." When Gabrielle tells Mother Emmanuel, "I just want to become a good nurse, and a good nun, and to do God's work wherever I am sent," Mother Emmanuel reminds her that her priorities are reversed. "First become a good nun," she says.

In the ceremony of vesture, the postulants enter the chapel of the convent dressed entirely in white, with flowered veils, like brides. Their hair is shorn, they are given new garments and, as in marriage, new names. Gaby is to be called Sister Luke. She is henceforth a novice.

Further instruction ensues. "Only as your pride slowly crumbles will you get the first glimpse of true humility," a new instructor-nun tells the novices. In this phase, the sisters must "in charity" denounce one another in chapel for observed imperfections. Another novice, to whom Sister Luke has grown close, denounces both herself and Sister Luke for seeking out each other's company and breaking the Grand Silence. In penance, the two novices must kiss the feet of the head nuns and scrub the convent floor. Subsequently, Sister Luke prays to God about her persistent imperfections: "When I succeed in obeying the Rule, I fail at the same time because I have pride in succeeding."

The night before the next stage of commitment, Sister Luke's friend informs her that she is leaving the convent, insisting that it would be hypocritical of her to make vows when her soul is in rebellion. Sister Luke, despite her own misgivings, signs a three-year contract the following day and her white veil is replaced by a black one. She proceeds to the School of Tropical Medicine in Antwerp.

Here, Sister Luke's reputation as Dr. Van der Mal's daughter precedes her. Her work is lavishly praised by the professor ("Your father's daughter. Excellent!") and he charges her to help another, older nun who is a less gifted scientist. Sister Luke discovers herself to be contemptuous of Sister Pauline, who is, in turn, jealous and disdainful of Sister Luke. The Reverend Mother Marcella of the convent in Antwerp counsels Sister Luke to fail her final examination as a way of demonstrating her humility. For Mother Marcella, the perfect union with God arrives through a moment of supreme selflessness, rather than a moment of supreme self-achievement.

When Sister Luke enters the examination room, her professor informs her that he will call her father immediately after the exam is ended and tell him the result. Sister Luke struggles to keep silent when the first question is posed, but—unable to repress her intellect and ability—she finally blurts out the correct answers.

Both Sister Pauline and Sister Luke pass the examination, but only Sister Pauline is sent to the Congo. Sister Luke is assigned to the staff of the convent's mental sanitorium in Brussels. Having passed fourth in a class of eighty, she flunked the test of her humility.

Sister Luke's task at the sanitorium is to spend eight to ten hours a day in the hydrotherapy room, where patients, submerged to the neck in closed cabinets of warm water, shriek and wail and beat their heels incessantly against the walls of their tubs. It is like a medieval representation of the Inferno.

At night, Sister Luke has charge of the most violent ward, where patients are locked up in separate cells. Although "forbidden to open the door of any of these cells unless there is another sister with her, or a practical helper," Sister Luke, without summoning aid, brings a glass of water to a schizophrenic woman (Colleen Dewhurst) who believes herself to be the Archangel Gabriel. The woman attacks and nearly kills her namesake (Gabrielle). Afterward, Sister Luke accuses herself of pride and "a sense of heroism." The Mother Superior of the sanitorium tells Sister Luke she is being too hard on herself; that she must bend a little or she will break. Sister Luke says she has her own rule: all or nothing.

In the following scene, Sister Luke takes her final vows. The priest says, "I declare you from today the bride of Jesus Christ, son of Almighty God. *Pater et Filius et Spiritus Sanctus*." He slips a gold wedding band on the fourth finger of her left hand. "My daughter," the Reverend Mother Emmanuel adds, "may God give you peace."

At last Sister Luke is permitted to go to the Congo. Once there, however, she learns that she has been assigned to the European hospital rather than to the native one. Recovering from her disappointment, she catches her reflection in a glass instrument case. Rather than immediately averting her eyes, she lingers to straighten her veil. Dr. Fortunati (Peter Finch), the cynical surgeon with whom she will be working, interrupts her indiscretion. "You will say six Ave's and a Pater Noster for that bit of vanity, Sister." When Fortunati asks her if she has ever before assisted at an operation, she replies arrogantly, "Yes. My father's Dr. Hubert Van der Mal." "Oh, I see," Fortunati says coolly. "You'll say another five Ave's and beg your soup for *that* little display of pride, Sister."

The Nun's Story. Sister Luke (Audrey Hepburn) exhibits her wedding dress, worn on the day she becomes a bride of Christ. Its resemblance to an ordinary wedding gown contributes to the film's formation of a parallel between religious and secular marriage.

Mother Mathilde cautions Sister Luke about Fortunati. "He is a genius and a devil" and works his nuns nearly to death. "I'm used to doctors," Sister Luke responds. "My father—" Once again she nearly commits the sin of pride. Mother Mathilde tells her she must leave the operating room as soon as her work is completed and never linger to discuss a case. "You will be tempted to, because he's a marvel. But remember, he is also a man, a bachelor, and—I'm afraid—a nonbeliever. Don't ever think for an instant, Sister, that your habit will protect you."

Sister Luke proceeds to "singularize" herself, making innovations in the organization of the native hospital staff which the local newspapers and drums publicize. Mother Mathilde complains to Sister Luke that she did not even bother to ask permission.

In another singular act, Sister Luke is forced to operate on the shattered leg of a priest when Dr. Fortunati is away, and she manages to save it from amputation. Later, Fortunati comes to her room to congratulate her, bringing an X-ray of the priest's leg as a souvenir. In the course of their conversation, he makes an issue of her "exhausting inner struggle." She replies emotionally that she is, at the moment, committing a sin merely by conversing with him alone in her room.

Sister Luke continues to drive herself, working over her microscope until after midnight and then rising before five to assist in the operating room. As a result, she contracts tuberculosis. Fortunati insists upon examining her. "You're never wrong but let's hope this time you are." Sister Luke protests that another nun should be summoned before Fortunati examines her, but he reminds her that her condition must be kept secret or she will be returned to Belgium. Sister Luke acquiesces. After confirming the diagnosis, Fortunati proposes to quarantine her in a treehouse and administer the gold treatment. Then he addresses himself to the cause of her illness:

> I'm going to tell you something about yourself, Sister. I've never worked with any other kind of nurse except nuns since I began. And you're not in the mold, Sister. You never will be. You're what's called a worldly nun—ideal for the public, ideal for the patients, but you see things your own way. You stick to your own ideas. You'll never be the kind of nun that your convent expects you to be. *That's* your illness. The TB is a by-product.

While Sister Luke is recuperating in the treehouse, Sister Aurelie comes to visit. She tells Sister Luke that Fortunati has insisted she be pampered. "Isn't it wonderful?" she cries, delighting vicariously in her friend's rare opportunity to be served instead of being a servant.

When Mother Mathilde comes to visit, Sister Luke chatters merrily about not having any imperfections to report. But in doing so, she unwittingly breaks the Grand Silence.

The Nun's Story. Dr. Fortunati (Peter Finch) witnesses the effects of Sister Luke's "exhausting inner struggle" to submit her indomitable spirit to the will of God.

By Christmas time, Sister Luke is completely recovered and returns to work at the hospital. One afternoon, a native enters one of the wards and brutally assaults Sister Aurelie. Although her skull is shattered by the native's club, before she dies she manages to guide her slayer out of the ward, since his presence there endangers the lives of her patients.

The black staff of the hospital are horrified by their tribesman's action and expect retribution on the part of the white missionaries. Sister Luke, however, displays the proper Christian response of mercy and forgiveness. But she is not able to sustain this response in subsequent scenes.

Sent back to Europe with a white patient who requires special care, her return to the Congo is postponed indefinitely by the outbreak of World War II. Although the nuns are instructed to remain neutral, Sister Luke tacitly supports the Belgian resistance to the Nazi invasion. "I cannot obey anymore," she confesses. When she receives word that her father has been killed by the Germans, she decides to leave the convent. She reports her feelings to a priest. He tells her that perhaps neutrality toward the Germans is too much to ask of herself. "It is not too much to ask," she retorts. "I simply cannot obey."

In the final sequence of the film, Sister Luke signs the papal documents which release her from her vows as a nun. Her dowry is returned. She is directed to a part of the convent where no one can view her and instructed to surrender her habit and adopt the clothes of a civilian. Under the stony gaze of a statue of Christ, she removes her gold wedding band.

When she is ready to depart, she presses a button and a door automatically unlocks. She swings the door wide and, passing beneath a cross in the windowed arch above the doorway, steps out into the street. The camera remains inside the convent, providing a lengthy contemplation of the open doorway to the outside world.

The Nun's Story begins and ends with a relinquishing of rings. In the course of the film, actual and symbolic marriages are shown to be ultimately the same, and are therefore equally antithetical to the nature and needs of Gabrielle Van der Mal. Although we are

The Nun's Story. Sister Luke visits with her father (Dean Jagger) after returning from the Belgian Congo. He is the pivotal part of a trinity (father, Fortunati, and God) which she worships but cannot obey. Until her father's death, Sister Luke struggles to accept male supremacy and to make peace with the culturally imposed limitations on herself as a woman.

never told why Gabrielle breaks her engagement to Jean, it seems reasonable to assume that her marriage would have precluded her working as a nurse in a Congo bush station and might even have precluded her being a nurse at all. And while we are never told why Gabrielle elects to join a convent, it seems equally reasonable to assume she does so in order to pursue a career as a Congo nurse. Thus, when the convent, too, comes between Gabrielle and her dream, first by keeping her from the Congo until she is "mature in the religious life," then by assigning her to the white European hospital instead of the black one, by never permitting her to work in a bush station, and by preventing her from returning to the Congo once she has come back to Europe, it seems logical and consistent that she will decide to leave it.

It can also be assumed that Gabrielle feels compelled to select between one sort of marriage and another, and that she cannot serve as a nurse in the Congo except as a nun.

In this way, the entire sociological surface text of the film can be accounted for, and a conclusion drawn about women's growing disenchantment with the demands and limitations of marriage which *The Nun's Story,* in its successful release in the latter half of the fifties, reflected.

However, *The Nun's Story* also offers a psychological subtext, which recomplicates the issue of Gabrielle's choices. For example, the surface text ignores the fact that Gabrielle confuses her father (and subsequently Fortunati) with God; that is, she worships a trinity in which father, lover, and God are conflated. This is established through a series of implicit comparisons and parallels. Fortunati, Gabrielle tells Mother Emmanuel, is "very close to God" when he operates. Her father, like Fortunati, is a master surgeon, which means he is also "close to God." Both father and Fortunati consider Gabrielle ill-suited to be a nun, and both offer her unacceptable alternatives: Van der Mal wants Gaby to marry Jean, and Fortunati indicates his willingness to take Jean's place. In other words, both men challenge her marriage to God, in essence competing with God like rivals. (That is why Fortunati is also likened to the devil.) God is Gabrielle's symbolic father, her symbolic husband and lover, and her symbolic savior. Fortunati is a potential lover-husband and her actual savior, miraculously (according to Van der Mal) curing Gaby of tuberculosis. The trinity is evoked when Gabrielle, after learning of Van der Mal's death, cries out, "Father . . . Father . . . Father" (with a dramatic musical accent after each cry) in such a way that it is impossible to determine whether she is calling to her actual father or to God. Finally, the death of one directly precipitates her "divorce" from the other.

The consequence of this confusion between father, lover, and God is that Gabrielle must relate to all three in a way that does not violate her relationship with any one of them. A normal marriage to a lover like Jean or Fortunati is prohibited, since sex with the lover cannot be distinguished from incest with the father, any more than worship of God can be distinguished from adulation of father or lover. The religious life, as it is portrayed in *The Nun's Story,* is well equipped to accommodate a father-complex, the unresolved fixation of a daughter upon a father. For it permits—indeed sanctifies—the marriage of symbolic father and daughter, while eliminating the possibility of incest.

In this new light, Gabrielle's rejection of Jean, her choice of the convent, and her eventual departure from religious life can be seen as functions of her relationship to her father, rather than the necessities of her commitment to a professional career in a sexist society. But, of course, the two are related.

Gabrielle's neurotic fixation on her father occurs because, on the one hand, he is her role model and on the other, she—unlike a son—is not permitted to emulate him, regardless of her capacity to do so. The closest she can come is to be a cloistered nurse, a doctor's assistant, although her operation on the priest's leg establishes her ability to be a surgeon in her own right. Because she is not permitted to self-actualize, to become that which she admires, she is relegated to the position of serving and worshipping that which she is not. This situation generates her rebellion, but her rebellion is tempered with guilt. For what right does she have to oppose the established order of existence, an order allegedly consecrated by God Almighty?

Gabrielle's surrender to the religious life is a way of "normalizing" herself. That she is not "normal" is subtly suggested in the film when Gabrielle encounters her namesake, Archangel Gabriel, a wild woman confined to a cell. Gabrielle stares into this woman's shining eyes and says, "One ought to be able to get through to someone like her"—that is, one ought to be able to "tame" that wild spirit. But when Gabrielle tries, she is nearly killed, just as she nearly dies trying to submit her spirit to the rules of the convent.

The convent depicted in *The Nun's Story* teaches women that they are "nothing" and encourages them to perceive the annihilation of the self as the ultimate spiritual achievement, a state of grace. Its lessons are taught by *female* role models, mother-substitutes who refer to younger nuns as "children" and "daughters." Gabrielle has no mother in the film, not even a memory of one or an explanation of her absence. Apparently, Gabrielle has grown up without instruction and guidance in humility, servitude, sacrifice, and obedience, the characteristics associated with traditional femininity. Mother Emmanuel, Mother Marcella, and Mother Mathilde, among others, fill the gap in Gabrielle's life. And because they accept their lot beatifically, they are unarguably awesome. As Marilyn French writes about housewives in *The Women's Room* (1977): [2]

> They did not complain, they did not insist, they did not demand, they did not seem to want anything. Mira, used to the egotistic male world with its endless "I" . . . was astonished by the selflessness of these women. . . . She listened and she heard their acceptance, their love, their selflessness, and for the first time in her life, she thought that women were great. . . . Brave they were. Brave and good humored and accepting, they picked up the dropped stitches and finished knitting something warm for someone else, letting their own teeth rot and skimping on clothes to pay Johnny's dentist bill, laying aside their desire like a crushed flower. . . .

Gabrielle never reneges on her admiration for the women who are able to be good nuns: they are the perfection of traditional womanhood, the glorious achievement of the old order. But once her father is dead, the reasons which have compelled her to follow their example are no longer operative. The death of Gabrielle's father, equivalent in her mind to the death of God, topples the male hierarchy which has held her in thrall. Psychologically free, she is able to tackle the sociological barriers in the outside world.

The fact that this moment of liberation occurs in the midst of World War II links it historically to the American movement toward female independence, which gained momentum in the forties. However, the final image of this distinctly *fifties* film is not one of liberation, but of the contemplation of an open door from *inside* the convent. For that was precisely the perspective of millions of American women as they viewed *The Nun's Story* in 1958, on the verge of revolt.

---

[2] (New York: Summit Books).

12

Androgyny, Anyone?

Some Like It Hot *(1959)*

The material suggests that we may say that many, if not all, of the personality traits which we have called masculine or feminine are as lightly linked to sex, as are the clothing, the manners, and the form of headdress that a society at a given period assigns to either sex.

Margaret Mead, Sex and Temperament in
Three Primitive Societies *(1935)*

Comedy is the best camouflage. And Billy Wilder's *Some Like It Hot* is a very funny film, in the same way that Stanley Kubrick's *Dr. Strangelove* is funny, with one critical difference. An audience watching *Dr. Strangelove* in 1963 knew it was laughing into the void. The subtitle of Kubrick's film is "How I Stopped Worrying and Learned to Love the Bomb." *Some Like It Hot,* on the other hand, has no self-conscious subtitle which says what the audience is laughing off. But if it did, it might be something like "How I Copped Out on the Whole Male Sex and Came to Appreciate Women."

Some Like It Hot giggles and guffaws its way from murder, mayhem, terror, treachery, corruption, unemployment, and callous indifference to a haven of sweet safety through the magic of a sex change. But the movie is not ultimately about transsexuality. It's about androgyny, the state of being both male and female.

It is a simpleminded generality that men are killers and women are creators; that the world men make is savage and the world women make is safe. But Wilder's film contends that it is true insofar as men have *made* it true, by repressing their natural psychic androgyny in the name of a pure masculine ideal. The consequence depicted in *Some Like It Hot* is a male world so predatory that the resumption of androgyny becomes a matter of life and death.

The movie begins in Chicago, 1929. A hearse is chased by police. Instead of a corpse, it carries bootleg booze to Mozzarella's Funeral Parlor, a front for a speakeasy owned by a gangster named Spats Columbo (George Raft). The password of the speakeasy is "I've come to grandma's funeral" and to get a good table, one identifies oneself as a pallbearer. Inside the speakeasy, only coffee is served: "Scotch coffee, Canadian coffee, sour mash coffee . . ." In other words, from the outset of the film, nothing is what it seems and death abounds.

Joe and Jerry (Tony Curtis and Jack Lemmon) are musicians in the speakeasy. It's the first job they've had in four months. Joe wants to bet their entire first week's salary at the dog races. He assures Jerry that, even if they lose, their job is going to last a long time. "Suppose it doesn't?" Jerry demands. "Jerry boy," Joe responds confidently, "suppose the stock market crashes, suppose Mary Pickford divorces Douglas Fairbanks, suppose the Dodgers leave Brooklyn . . . ?" Following this accidental string of prophecies, the Chicago police (led by Pat O'Brien) raid the speakeasy, and Joe and Jerry are out of a job.

Joe decides they should pawn their overcoats and bet the money on a "sure thing" named Greased Lightning. In the next scene, they are without overcoats in the midst of a Chicago blizzard.

They proceed down a hallway of booking agents, seeking work. "Anything today?" "Nothing." Jerry says, "I can't go on, Joe. I'm weak from hunger, I'm running a fever, I've got a hole in my shoe . . ." When they reach Sid Poliakoff's office, a secretary named Nellie greets them with outrage. It seems Joe—"What a heel!"—made

Some Like It Hot. Spats Columbo (George Raft) averts his eyes as his "boys" enact the St. Valentine's Day Massacre. This image of men making death on a day designated for love suggests in miniature the nature of the male world which the two protagonists of the film flee.

a date with Nellie and then stood her up. After Joe fabricates an excuse, and Jerry corroborates it, they beg Nellie for a job. In revenge, Nellie sends them into Poliakoff's office on a wild-goose chase.

Sweet Sue and her Society Syncopators are looking for a tenor sax and bass for a three-week engagement in Florida, but while Joe and Jerry play the right instruments, they don't meet the other requirements for the job. "You gotta be under twenty-five," Poliakoff explains. "We could pass for that," Jerry insists. "You gotta be blond," Poliakoff adds. "We could dye our hair," Jerry offers. "You gotta be girls!" Poliakoff concludes. "We could—" Jerry begins, but Joe cuts him off. "No, we couldn't!" Poliakoff offers them a one-night stand at a St. Valentine's Day dance in Urbana, a hundred miles away. In desperation they accept. Joe then tricks Nellie into lending them her car. But when they go to pick up the automobile at Nellie's garage, they accidentally witness the St. Valentine's Day Massacre, staged by Spats Columbo as vengeance on Toothpick Charlie for squealing to the police and thereby prompting the raid on Spats's speakeasy.

Miraculously, Joe and Jerry escape the gangsters' machine guns, but not before Spats and his gang have had a good long look at them and their instrument cases. Now they are Columbo's targets and must get out of town.

In the next scene, Joe and Jerry appear at the train station in full drag, complete with stiletto heels. "How do they walk in these things?" Jerry demands as they wobble toward the train. "How do they keep their balance?" Then he complains that dresses are "drafty," and muses that women "must be catching cold all the time." Finally, he exclaims, "I feel naked! . . . I feel like everybody's staring at me."

A beautiful blonde passes them, taking her femininity for granted. "Look at that! Look how she moves. It's just like Jell-O on springs," Jerry comments. "I tell you, it's a whole different sex!" Joe retorts, "What are you afraid of? Nobody's asking you to have a baby."

They report to Sweet Sue and her manager, a milquetoast named Bienstock. "We're the new girls," Joe says. "Brand-new," Jerry adds. They introduce themselves as Josephine and Daphne (a sudden inspiration on Jerry's part, since he was supposed to be called Geraldine). Bienstock says they've saved his life. "Likewise, I'm sure," Josephine replies.

In the ladies room of the train, Josephine and Daphne reencounter the beautiful blonde, sneaking a drink. She is Sugar Kane, nee Sugar Kowalchek (Marilyn Monroe), the singer in Sweet Sue's band. She tells the "girls" that she's only with this particular band because she's "running away." By way of explanation, she says that she always gets the "fuzzy end of the lollipop."

Later, as the band is rehearsing, Sugar's whiskey flask slips out of her garter and falls to the floor of the train. Before Sugar can be fired, Daphne claims the flask as "her" own. Sweet Sue explains that she does not permit liquor or men during working hours. Daphne

Some Like It Hot. Daphne (Jack Lemmon) and Sugar (Marilyn Monroe) frolic on the beach in Florida, where Sugar has come to meet a millionaire. Sugar is Daphne's female role model, as their blond hair and similar swim suits suggest. But it is Daphne, not Sugar, who will snag a *real* millionaire.

replies, "We wouldn't be caught dead with men. Rough hairy beasts! Eight hands! And they all just want one thing from a girl!" "I beg your pardon, miss!" Bienstock interjects indignantly.

When everyone is asleep, Sugar, wearing a sheer black nightgown, crawls into Daphne's bunk to thank "her" for laying claim to the whiskey flask. They cuddle affectionately, although Jerry is nearly beside himself with sexual temptation. Sugar confides, "When I was a little girl, on cold nights like this, I used to crawl into bed with my sister. We'd cuddle up under the covers and pretend we were lost in a dark cave and were trying to find our way out." Jerry decides to turn their cuddle into a surprise party (his true sexual identity the surprise), but when he goes to get some whiskey to soften the blow, he wakes some of the girls and before long the entire band is crammed into Daphne's bunk.

The noise wakes Josephine. "She" follows Sugar into the ladies room, where Sugar has gone to chop ice for drinks. Sugar tells "her" the story of her life with men:

> I used to sing with male bands but I can't afford it anymore. . . . That's what I'm running away from. I've worked with six different ones in the last two years. Oh, brother!

Sugar confesses that she has no resistance against tenor saxophone players. When Josephine reminds her that "she" plays tenor sax, Sugar replies,

> But you're a girl, thank goodness . . . That's why I joined this band. Safety first. Anything to get away from those bums. . . . You don't know what they're like. You fall for them, you really love them, you think this is going to be the biggest thing since the Graf Zeppelin. The next thing you know, they're borrowing money from you, they're spending it on other dames, and betting on horses. . . . Then one morning you wake up, the guy's gone, the saxophone's gone, all that's left behind is a pair of old socks and a tube of toothpaste—all squeezed out. So—you pull yourself together, you go on to the next job, the next saxophone player; it's the same thing all over again. . . . I can tell you one thing. It's not going to happen to me again, ever. I'm tired of getting the fuzzy end of the lollipop.

Sugar intends to catch a millionaire in Florida, one who wears glasses. "Men who wear glasses are so much more gentle, sweet, and helpless," she explains. "I hope this time you wind up with the—sweet end of the lollipop," Josephine says.

The band arrives in Florida and takes up residence at the Seminole Ritz Hotel, its porch lined with elderly millionaires, including Osgood Fielding III (Joe E. Brown). Osgood expresses appreciation for all the girls who pass, but when he sees Daphne, he is smitten ("Zowee!") and follows "her" to the elevator. Riding up, Osgood makes a pass. "What kind of a girl do you think I am, Mr. Fielding," Daphne indignantly demands, and slaps him sharply across the face. At the same time, Josephine is harassed by the bellboy, an obnoxious little adolescent who likes women "big and sassy."

Jerry enters the hotel room disgruntled. "Dirty old man. . . . I just got pinched in the elevator." "Well, now you know how the other half lives," Joe replies. "I'm not even pretty," Jerry says, looking at himself in a mirror. "They don't care," Joe responds, "just so long as you're wearing a skirt. It's like waving a red flag in front of a bull." "Well, I'm sick of being a flag," Jerry says. "I want to be a bull again."

Joe explains that they can't leave Sweet Sue's. They're broke and if they join a *male* band, Spats will be sure to find them. "So you got pinched in the elevator. So what! Would you rather be picking lead out of your navel? . . . What's the beef? We're sitting pretty. We've got room and board, we're getting paid every week . . ." Jerry jealously accuses Joe of wanting to stay with the band because of Sugar. "I saw you, the both of you, in that bus, all lovey-dovey and whispering and giggling and borrowing each other's lipstick. I saw you!" Joe vigorously denies Jerry's allegation. "What are you talking about? We're just like sisters."

But in fact, Jerry is correct. Joe steals Bienstock's glasses and suitcase full of foppish yachting clothes and goes off to the beach disguised as Sugar's mild-mannered millionaire. They meet and Sugar is ecstatic ("Well, he's young and he's handsome. He's a bachelor. He's a real gentleman. You know—not one of these grabbers," she tells Josephine and Daphne), but Jerry is disgusted. After Sugar has gone off, he demands, "What are you trying to do to that poor girl, putting on a millionaire act! . . . Joe, I've seen you pull some low tricks on women. This is without doubt the trickiest, lowest, and meanest . . ."

Osgood invites Daphne to have dinner with him on his yacht. Joe accepts on Jerry's behalf, and then insists that Jerry keep Osgood on shore so that he can play millionaire with Sugar on Osgood's yacht. Osgood and Daphne go tango dancing. On the yacht, Joe seduces Sugar by pretending to be impotent so that *she* can seduce *him*. "Girls leave me cold," he says, but Sugar changes all that. At dawn the couples return to the hotel. Jerry announces to Joe that he's engaged. "Congratulations!" Joe says, "Who's the lucky girl?" "I am," Jerry replies.

Joe: What are you talking about? You can't marry Osgood.
Jerry: Do you think he's too old for me?
Joe: Jerry, you can't be serious!
Jerry: Why not? He's marrying girls all the time!
Joe: But you're not a girl, you're a guy. And why would a guy want to marry a guy?
Jerry: Security. . . . I'm not stupid. I know there's a problem.
Joe: I'll say there is.
Jerry: His mother. We need her approval. But I'm not worried because I don't smoke.
Joe: Jerry, there's *another* problem. Like what are you going to do on your honeymoon?
Jerry: We've been discussing that. He wants to go to the Riviera, but I kinda lean toward Niagara Falls.

Joe persuades Jerry that he *can't* marry Osgood, and that they should pawn Osgood's engagement present—a diamond bracelet—for financial independence.

"I feel like such a tramp, taking jewelry from a man under false pretenses," Jerry says later as they are walking through the lobby of the hotel. Then he eyes Spats and his cronies in the mirror of his compact. The "girls" beat a hasty retreat to the elevator, but the gangsters follow them and try to pick them up. Haven't they met somewhere before, in Chicago, perhaps?—the gangsters inquire. "We wouldn't be caught dead in Chicago," the "girls" reply.

They return to their room and pack their suitcases for a quick getaway. Jerry laments leaving Osgood. Joe says he must say good-bye to Sugar. "We can't just walk out on her without saying good-bye." "What? Since when?" Jerry demands. "You usually walk out and leave 'em with nothing but a kick in the teeth." "That's when I was a saxophone player," Joe replies. "Now I'm a millionaire."

Joe fakes a ship-to-shore phone call to Sugar and tells her he's leaving permanently for the oil fields of Venezuela. In a moment of guilty generosity, he slides Jerry's diamond bracelet across the hall to Sugar's door. Sugar finds the bracelet, returns to the phone, and asks, "Are you always this generous?" "Not always," Joe says soberly.

The gangsters spot Joe and Jerry climbing down the balconies from their room and give chase. The "ladies" change costume, emerg-

Some Like It Hot. In the guise of Josephine, Joe (Tony Curtis) really listens to Sugar and learns for the first time what it means to be a woman in a man's world. Sugar, in turn, trusts Josephine with the truth about herself, which she would never reveal to a man. Their female bond is maintained even after Sugar discovers that Josephine is a man.

ing as a bellboy and an old man in a wheelchair, but Jerry's high heels give them away and the chase resumes. They race into a convention dining room and hide beneath the banquet table. As fate would have it, the entire hoodlum empire, headed by "Little Bonaparte," enters and is seated. "Little Bonaparte" has arranged a surprise party for Spats to commemorate the death of Toothpick Charlie. During the second chorus of "For He's a Jolly Good Fellow," a man leaps out of a cake and machine-guns Spats and his cohorts to death. In this way, Joe and Jerry accidentally witness their second gangland mass murder.

Joe decides the only way they can escape is on Osgood's yacht. They change back into ladies' clothes and Jerry goes off to call Osgood. In the meantime, Joe watches Sugar sing "I'm Through with Love." Moved by Sugar's sadness, he goes to her at the end of her song and, in front of everyone and in full drag, kisses her on the mouth. "None of that, Sugar," he murmurs. "No guy is worth it." Sugar, along with everyone else, suddenly realizes Josephine is a man.

The chase continues, but now Sugar is part of it, following Joe and Jerry down to the dock. All three leap into Osgood's motorboat and set off for the yacht.

"You don't want me, Sugar," Joe says. "I'm a liar and a phony. A saxophone player! One of those no-goodniks you keep running away from." But Sugar can't be dissuaded, so Joe finally gives in and kisses her.

Osgood tells Daphne that his mother wants "her" to be married in the mother's wedding dress. Daphne says "she" can't: "She and I—we are not built the same way."

> *Osgood:* We can have it altered.
> *Jerry:* Oh, no, you don't. Osgood, I'm gonna level with you.
> We can't get married at all.
> *Osgood:* Why not?
> *Jerry:* Well, in the first place, I'm not a natural blond.
> *Osgood:* It doesn't matter.
> *Jerry:* I smoke—I smoke all the time.
> *Osgood:* I don't care.

Jerry: I have a terrible past. For three years now, I've been living with a saxophone player.
Osgood: I forgive you.
Jerry: I can never have children.
Osgood: We can adopt some.
Jerry: You don't understand, Osgood. (*He pulls off his wig*) Aw—I'm a man.
Osgood: Well—nobody's perfect.

Some Like It Hot flirts with a whole range of taboo sexual topics: transsexuality, homosexuality, bisexuality, transvestism, lesbianism, oral sex (the sweet and fuzzy ends of the lollipop), and impotence. The characters shift from one sort of sexuality to another with the fluidity of a cartoon or a dream, while always maintaining their innocence on the literal (or waking) level. In one sense, this "normal" level is a dodge, a camouflage, a way of denying the reality of the various sexual "deviations" in order to preserve the film's comic veneer. But if one is willing to allow that all forms of sexuality (and asexuality) have at least a psychic life in the subconscious mind of every so-called normal person (e.g., a man's fantasy of having a baby, a heterosexual woman's fleeting image of making love to another woman, a man's fear of impotence), then the film can be perceived in part as a good-natured dream of sexuality as a sliding scale from male to female, from straight to gay, from potent to impotent, on which every human being dances an endlessly variable jig.

This dream is juxtaposed with the nightmare of the gangster world, saturated with the imagery of violence and death: gunfire, screeching tires, sirens, a hearse, a funeral parlor, screams, frenetic jazz, and human slaughter. The title of the film is a reference to jazz and the hot male world from which it emanates. "Oh, well, I guess some like it hot," the millionaire says to Sugar. "I personally prefer classical music."

Spats, a composite of famous movie gangsters from the past, is the center of a hoodlum fraternity which has eschewed sex for violence. Like the protagonist of *Little Caesar* (1930), Spats is obsessed with upward mobility. It is his plan to replace Little Bonaparte, who "used to be like a rock" but is "getting soft." Softness is so threatening to Spats and Little Caesar that they have nothing whatsoever to do with women. The famous scene from *Public Enemy* (1931), in which James Cagney shoves a grapefruit into Mae Marsh's face, is duplicated in *Some Like It Hot* with Spats and a *male* crony. Spats's attitude toward women is also suggested, indirectly, by his compulsive attention to his snowy white spats, his insistence that his aides only touch them with clean hands, and his horror when blood drips onto them at one point in the film. The sense that sex (and women) are dirty is often expressed as an obsession with cleanliness and purity.

Joe and, to a lesser extent, Jerry live on the fringes of this male fraternity. They both work for Spats, play jazz, and perceive women as exploitable sex objects. They have borrowed money, according to Jerry, from every dancer at the speakeasy. They lie to Nellie about why Joe stood her up, and they hustle her for a job. But it is Joe who initiates all the bad behavior. He tricks Nellie into lending her car and is about to charge gasoline to her account when the massacre occurs. Later, Sugar's stories about saxophone players, together with Jerry's reminiscences about Joe's lack of character ("You usually walk out and leave 'em with nothing but a kick in the teeth"), complete the picture. Joe is a "heel," a "bum," a "no-goodnik" in relation to women.

But after witnessing the St. Valentine's Day Massacre—men slaughtering men on a day set aside for the celebration of love—Joe is forced to seek refuge in the opposite sex. Like Sugar, he is running away from men, so he comes to understand "how the other half lives," and how they perceive men. "You don't know what they're like," Sugar says. When she tells Josephine her stories—"Two in the morning he sent me down for hotdogs and potato salad. They were out of potato salad so I brought cole slaw. So he threw it right in my face"—Joe must confront the consequences of his own cavalier behavior: the fear, the sadness, the drinking, the self-denigration. As a "woman" friend, Joe gets to know the *real* Sugar, not "sugar and spice and everything nice" but Sugar Kowalchek from Sandusky, Ohio, a vulnerable and lovable human being. As Joe the saxophone player, he wouldn't know Sugar at

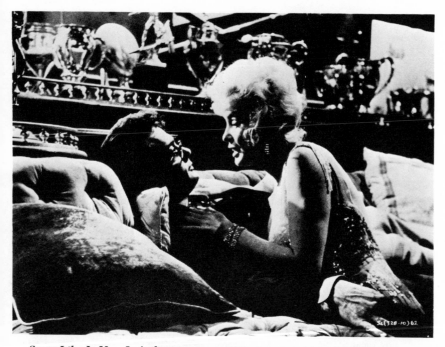

Some Like It Hot. Joe's disguise as a millionaire gives him and Sugar an opportunity to experience different facets of themselves. Joe becomes an impotent and helpless benefactor; Sugar becomes the aggressor, seducing *him.* This reversal of traditional roles paves the way for a more equalized relationship.

all. Even as the millionaire, Joe learns nothing true about Sugar, except that she is affectionate, because Sugar lies to impress him, telling him she's a society girl on a lark. She reveals none of the sad accounts of her past, nor her vulnerability in the present. The real millionaire wouldn't see Sugar after he had brushed her off. But when Sugar comes across the hallway to tell Josephine about the phone call, Joe must once again witness the consequences of his actions from his own female perspective. This awareness alienates Joe from his own sex to such an extent that, even early on, he refers to men as "they." ("They don't care," he tells Jerry, "just so long as you're wearing a skirt.")

As a woman Joe comes to appreciate what Sugar wants in a man: someone "gentle, sweet, and helpless," someone who will give her something instead of just taking. And because Joe wants to give her "the sweet end of the lollipop" for a change, he tries to become her ideal man. But in fact, the millionaire isn't ideal; he's merely a transition Joe must experience on his way to becoming a human being. The millionaire is everything Joe is not—financially independent and emotionally dependent, passive, and impotent. Sugar must "go after *him*," seduce *him*. This gives Sugar the power and control over a man she's never had before, and so the millionaire also provides a transition for *her*. This transitional relationship, however, does not permit either character to be *real*, only different.

In their ultimate relationship, Joe renounces both the millionaire and the saxophone player ("No guy is worth it"; "You don't want me, Sugar") while affirming the "female" bond between them by kissing her, as Josephine, on the mouth and maintaining his female clothing and makeup to the end of the movie. Sugar, in turn, retains a measure of her new aggressiveness (she pursues Joe down to Osgood's boat) and renounces her fantasy of the "ideal" weak millionaire in favor of the real but renovated Joe.

Jerry, unlike Joe, is androgynous from the outset of the film, but he doesn't know it. His relationship with Osgood is actually no more than an exaggeration (and an improvement) of his relationship with Joe. In both instances, Jerry plays the "female" role, as he suggests in his confession to Osgood: "I have a terrible past. For three years now, I've been living with a saxophone player." As a "woman," Jerry is conned, dominated, and ripped off by Joe: Joe persuades him to hock his overcoat in the middle of winter; Joe decides they will disguise themselves as women and take the Florida job (although Jerry suggested the idea in the first place); and Joe steals Jerry's flowers and his diamond bracelet and gives them to Sugar; he even appropriates Osgood's yacht. Jerry, in turn, is Joe's feminine conscience, calling him on his reprehensible behavior toward women.

Because of Jerry's predisposition to femininity, he develops a much more complete female persona than Joe. Rather than merely feminizing his male name to Geraldine, he imaginatively selects an entirely new name—Daphne. Moreover, he is concerned with his female impersonation in a way that Joe is not. He watches Sugar like a role model ("Look at that. Look how she moves.") and eventually attracts the millionaire Sugar hopes to meet. Finally, he forgets that he is "a boy" and begins to think of himself as a woman.

For Jerry, being a woman provides the security he doesn't have as a man. It goes beyond the immediate danger of Spats; Jerry wants to divest himself entirely of the burdens of being male. (When he first meets Osgood, Jerry unloads on him all the suitcases and instruments he has been carrying into the hotel.) Although he laments the indignities of being a woman, he also perceives the advantages, *if* one is lucky enough to land a good man. "I tell you, I will never find another man who's so good to me," he says to Joe about Osgood, and when Joe is surprised that the diamonds in Jerry's engagement bracelet are genuine, Jerry retorts, "Of course they're real! What do you think, my fiancé's a bum?"

While it is possible to argue that Jerry is simply gay, and that his relationship with Osgood is homosexual, it is equally valid to see Jerry's feminization as the expression of a "normal" male's longing for passivity and dependence, which even the more virile Joe adopts in his portrayal of the millionaire. Certainly, American films of the late forties and fifties are sufficiently rife with examples of this heterosexual male helplessness to justify this interpretation.[1] As Robert Warshow writes about *The Best Years of Our Lives* (1946),

> . . . the sexual relations of the characters form an unusually clear projection of the familiar Hollywood (and American) dream of male passivity. The men are inept, nervous, inarticulate, and childishly willful. . . . the [handless] sailor's misfortune becomes a kind of wish-fulfillment, as one might

---

[1] Billy Wilder's own *Sunset Boulevard* is an example. Male helplessness and passivity also play a part in *The Marrying Kind, Shane, The Country Girl, All That Heaven Allows,* and *Picnic.*

actually dream it: he *must* be passive; therefore he can be passive without guilt.[2]

Whether one perceives Jerry as straight or gay, what *Some Like It Hot* affirms is neither heterosexual nor homosexual, nor even female, but rather, the abolition of those absolute poles in favor of an androgynous continuum which each of the three main characters explores in search of a uniquely suitable sexual identity. Sugar and Daphne cuddle in a train berth like sexually curious sisters "lost in [the] dark cave" of their own female bodies; Josephine and Sugar eventually have a lesbian embrace. Jerry and Joe both court Sugar as male suitors, although Jerry never has the chance to give her his surprise party. Josephine is pursued by a bellboy; Daphne by Osgood. Joe is both a virile stud and an impotent fop. Sugar is both passive and aggressive, the seduced victim and the seducer-victor ("Here you are, making a chump out of all those experts!" the millionaire tells Sugar when she finally succeeds in turning him on). And all of this harmless sexual exploration is placed in innocent opposition to the fixed obscenity of violence and death that the "pure male" of the film represents.

Alfred Hitchcock's *Psycho* (1960) appears to be a reversal of that vision. It depicts an androgynous psychopath whose violence derives from his inability to reconcile the male and female aspects of his personality. Norman Bates stabilizes only at the point where Norman-mother becomes entirely mother. But in fact, what underlies the film is the terror of female dominance (a psychiatrist explains that "mother" was the dominant part of Norman's personality and therefore eventually won out) which androgyny might allow.

Some Like It Hot and *Psycho* represent in microcosm the opposing poles of cultural feeling about the revolution in sex roles that was fomenting throughout the fifties and which erupted in the sixties.

* * * * * * * *

The timid, tentative, camouflaged emancipation of the fifties appears primitive and token in comparison to the practical realities and

---

[2] *The Immediate Experience* (New York: Atheneum, 1970).

theoretical considerations of women's liberation in the seventies. It is hardly more than an angry outburst against a dimly perceived injustice, and often it is less than that. What it never becomes is a perception beyond the personal, and so it is presented as a series of problems which are resolvable in personal, or interpersonal, terms: in the renewed marital contract of the Chester Keefers in *The Marrying Kind,* or the solitary abandonment of the convent by Sister Luke in *The Nun's Story.* But the personal solution, divorced from the larger social, political, and economic dilemma, is doomed because it is impotent. It must continually bend and bow to the reactionary power of the establishment, with which it inevitably comes to grips. Mrs. Chester Keefer remains married and returns to work in 1952, but her job as a secretary is a low-paying dead-end. She is merely a source of cheap labor to her boss and a source of supplementary income to her family. Her real job still awaits her at home: the shopping, cooking, cleaning, childraising, and husband nurturing of the homemaker. In both her work and her home, she has responsibility without authority, duty without power or prestige. She is still a servant to a husband obsessed with material success. She is still a second-class citizen.

But Mrs. Keefer is nonetheless privileged in comparison to America's poor white and minority women. No commercially significant film in the fifties is addressed to them. It is as if they do not exist in the imaginative consciousness of the culture, except as housekeepers in the immaculate middle-class homes of others. There is, for example, a black maid in *Rebel Without a Cause* (1955) who cries over the body of a dead white teenager whom she has raised for an absentee white mother. But all the critical attention of the film is directed at the plight of the middle class. There is a poor white housekeeper in *Peyton Place* (1957) who hangs herself after discovering that her husband has raped her daughter. But even though we see the squalor and misery of this woman's life, they are presented without any political or economic context, and so become merely a sensationalized instance of local color.

There is also no opportunity in films of the fifties to wonder if women should *want* to assume power in a dehumanizing technocratic society. No doubt, women like Norma in *Sunset Boulevard,* Mary

Kate in *The Quiet Man,* Georgie in *The Country Girl,* and Sister Luke in *The Nun's Story* have the capacity to assume men's roles in the working world; no doubt, they are the equals of male megalomaniacs and workaholics. But what is the *human* advantage of an ambisexual power elite based on ruthless competition and exploitation? And if the answer is that there is no advantage, then women must be prepared to change a great deal more than their status. They must change the system in which status is conferred.

America in the fifties was on the verge of a revolution which challenged many of the fundamental ordering principles of western culture: not only male supremacy, but white supremacy, and an economic system in which one sector of society benefits at the expense of another. The sixties appeared to be the fulfillment of that revolutionary promise, the answer to all the questions which the fifties raised—or ignored. But the seventies have shown us that the ball has only just begun to roll—and that it can roll backward as well as forward.

Selected Bibliography

Amberg, George, ed. *The New York Times Film Reviews 1913–1970: A One-Volume Selection.* New York: Arno Books, 1971.

Banner, Lois W. *Women in Modern America: A Brief History.* New York: Harcourt, Brace, Jovanovich, 1974.

de Beauvoir, Simone. *The Second Sex.* Tr. and ed. H. M. Parshley. New York: Bantam Books, 1961.

Bird, Caroline. *Born Female: The High Cost of Keeping Women Down.* New York: Pocket Books, 1969.

Chesler, Phyllis. *Women and Madness.* New York: Avon Books, 1972.

Dowdy, Andrew. *The Films of the Fifties: The American State of Mind.* New York: William Morrow, 1975; originally pub. as *Movies Are Better Than Ever: Wide Screen Memories of the Fifties.*

Eisinger, Chester E. "Focus on Arthur Miller's *Death of a Salesman:* The Wrong Dreams." *American Dreams, American Nightmares.* Ed. David Madden. Carbondale and Edwardsville: Southern Illinois Univ. Press, 1972.

Fiedler, Leslie A. *Love and Death in the American Novel.* Cleveland and New York: Meridian Books, 1962.

Von Franz, Marie-Louise. *The Feminine in Fairy Tales.* Zurich: Spring Publications, 1973.

———. *An Introduction to the Psychology of Fairy Tales.* Zurich: Spring Publications, 1973.

French, Marilyn. *The Women's Room.* New York: Summit Books, 1977.

Friedan, Betty. *The Feminine Mystique.* New York: Dell, 1963.

Goldberg, Herbert. *The Hazards of Being Male: Surviving the Myth of Masculine Privilege.* New York: New American Library, 1977.

Goldman, Eric F. *The Crucial Decade—and After: America, 1945–60.* New York: Vintage Books, 1960.

Gorer, Geoffrey. *The American People: A Study in National Character.* Rev. ed. New York: W. W. Norton, 1964.

Gow, Gordon. *Hollywood in the Fifties.* New York: A. S. Barnes & Co.; London: A. Zwemmer Ltd., 1971.

Halliday, Jon. *Sirk on Sirk.* New York: Viking Press, 1972.

Hardwick, Elizabeth. *Seduction and Betrayal: Women and Literature.* New York: Vintage, 1975.

Haskell, Molly. *From Reverence to Rape: The Treatment of Women in the Movies.* Baltimore: Penguin Books, 1974.

Hofstadter, Richard. *Anti-Intellectualism in American Life.* New York: Vintage, 1963.

Horney, Karen. *Feminine Psychology.* New York: W. W. Norton, 1967.

Hulme, Kathryn. *The Nun's Story.* New York: Pocket Books, 1958.

Inge, William. *Picnic. Best American Plays: Fourth Series 1951–1957.* New York: Crown, 1958.

Jones, James. *From Here to Eternity.* New York: Avon Books, 1975.

Kay, Karen, and Peary, Gerald, eds. *Women and the Cinema: A Critical Anthology.* New York: E. P. Dutton, 1977.

Lawrence, D. H. *Studies in Classic American Literature.* Garden City, New York: Anchor Books, 1951.

Lerner, Gerda. *The Female Experience: An American Documentary.* Indianapolis: Bobbs-Merrill, 1977.

Lifton, Robert Jay. "Woman as Knower: Some Psychohistorical Perspectives." *The Woman in America.* Ed. Robert Jay Lifton. Boston: Beacon Press, 1967.

Lowen, Alexander. *The Betrayal of the Body.* London: Collier MacMillan, Ltd., 1969.

MacCann, Richard Dyer, ed. *Film and Society.* New York: Charles Scribner's Sons, 1964.

Mailer, Norman. *Marilyn: A Biography.* New York: Grosset & Dunlap, 1973.

———. *The Deer Park.* New York: Berkley Windhover, 1976.

Matthiessen, F. O. "Book One: From Emerson to Thoreau." *American Renaissance: Art and Expression in the Age of Emerson and Whitman.* London, Oxford, and New York: Oxford Univ. Press, 1968.

McClelland, David C. "Wanted: A New Self-Image for Women." *The Woman in America.* Ed. Robert Jay Lifton. Boston: Beacon Press, 1967.

McConnell, Frank D. *The Spoken Seen: Film and the Romantic Imagination.* Baltimore and London: Johns Hopkins Univ. Press, 1975.

Mellen, Joan. *Women and Their Sexuality in the New Film.* New York: Dell, 1973.

Miller, Arthur. *Death of a Salesman.* New York: Viking, 1958.

Miller, Douglas T., and Nowak, Marion. *The Fifties: The Way We Really Were.* Garden City, New York: Doubleday, 1977.

Murray, Henry A., ed. *Myth and Mythmaking.* Boston: Beacon Press, 1968.

Powdermaker, Hortense. *Hollywood: The Dream Factory.* Boston: Little, Brown, 1950.

Rosen, Marjorie. *Popcorn Venus.* New York: Avon Books, 1974.

Rossi, Alice S. "Equality Between the Sexes: An Immodest Proposal." *The Woman in America.* Ed. Robert Jay Lifton. Boston: Beacon Press, 1967.

Roszak, Betty, and Roszak, Theodore, eds. *Masculine/Feminine: Readings in Sexual Mythology and the Liberation of Women.* New York: Harper and Row, 1969.

Rourke, Constance. "The Roots of American Culture." *The Roots of American Culture and Other Essays.* New York: Harvest Books, 1942.

Ryan, Mary P. *Womanhood in America: From Colonial Times to the Present.* New York: New Viewpoints, 1975.

Sayers, Dorothy. *Unpopular Opinions.* New York: Harcourt, Brace and World, 1947.

Schorer, Mark. "Technique as Discovery," "Fiction and the Analogical Matrix," and *"Emma." The World We Imagine.* New York: Farrar, Straus, and Giroux, 1968.

Sklar, Robert. *Movie-Made America: A Cultural History of American Movies.* New York: Vintage, 1976.

Slater, Philip E. *The Glory of Hera: Greek Mythology and the Greek Family.* Boston: Beacon Press, 1968.

Smith, Henry Nash. "The Western Hero in the Dime Novel," "The Dime Novel Heroine," "The Garden of the World and American Agrarianism," and "The Garden and the Desert." *Virgin Land.* Cambridge, Mass.: Harvard Univ. Press, 1970.

Walker, Alexander. *Stardom: The Hollywood Phenomenon.* New York: Stein and Day, 1970.

Warshow, Robert. *The Immediate Experience: Movies, Comics, Theater & Other Aspects of Popular Culture.* New York: Atheneum, 1970.

Weibel, Kathryn. *Mirror Mirror: Images of Women Reflected in Popular Culture.* New York: Anchor Books, 1977.

Welsch, Janice Rita. *An Analysis of the Film Images of Hollywood's Most Popular Post-WWII Female Stars.* Dissertation, Northwestern University, 1975. Ann Arbor: University Microfilms, 1976.

Wolfenstein, Martha, and Leites, Nathan. *Movies: A Psychological Study.* New York: Atheneum, 1970.

Wood, Michael. *America in the Movies* (or "Santa Maria, It Had Slipped My Mind"). New York: Delta, 1976.

Ziff, Larzer. "The Midwestern Imagination" and "Overcivilization: Harold Frederic, The Roosevelt-Adams Outlook, Owen Wister." *The American 1890's: Life and Times of a Lost Generation.* New York: Viking, 1966.

Film Rental Information (16 mm.)[1]

Sunset Boulevard: 110 minutes, black and white. Distributed by Films
   Incorporated.
The Quiet Man: 129 minutes, color. Distributed by Ivy Film.
The Marrying Kind: 96 minutes, black and white. Distributed by Audio
   Brandon Films (Macmillan) and Institutional Cinema Service, Inc.
Shane: 117 minutes, color. Distributed by Films Incorporated.
From Here to Eternity: 118 minutes, black and white. Distributed by
   Audio Brandon Films, Arcus Films, Inc., Budget Films, Cine Craft
   Company, Clem Williams Films, Inc., Contemporary/McGraw Hill
   Films, "The" Film Center, Institutional Cinema Service, Inc.,
   Twyman Films, Inc., and Wholesome Film Center.
The Country Girl: 104 minutes, black and white. Distributed by Films,
   Incorporated.
The Tender Trap: 111 minutes, color. Distributed by Films, Incorporated.
Marty: 91 minutes, black and white. Distributed by United Artists 16.
All That Heaven Allows: 89 minutes, color. Distributed by Universal 16.
Picnic: 115 minutes, color. Distributed by Audio Brandon Films (Mac-
   millan), Budget Films, Clem Williams Films, Inc., Institutional
   Cinema Service, Inc.
Heaven Knows, Mr. Allyson: 107 minutes, color. Distributed by Films,
   Incorporated.
The Nun's Story: 151 minutes, color. Distributed by Audio Brandon
   Films, Arcus Films, Inc., Cine Craft Company, Budget Films,
   National Film Service, Twyman Films, Inc., Trans-World Films,
   Inc., and United Films.
Some Like It Hot: 121 minutes, black and white. Distributed by United
   Artists 16.

---

[1] Information derived from *Film Programmer's Guide to 16 MM. Rentals:*
Second edition, compiled and edited by Kathleen Weaver (Berkeley, Calif.:
Reel Research, 1975).

Distributors' Directory

Arcus Films, Inc.
  1225 Broadway
  New York, New York 10001
  (212) 686-2216
  1021 Columbia Avenue
  Atlanta, Georgia 30309
  (404) 892-0194

Audio Brandon Films (Macmillan)
  34 MacQuesten Parkway So.
  Mount Vernon, New York
    10550
  (914) 664-5051
  8400 Brookfield Avenue
  Brookfield, Illinois 60513
  (312) 485-3925
  3868 Piedmont
  Oakland, California 94611
  (415) 658-9890
  1619 N. Cherokee
  Los Angeles, California 90028
  (213) 463-0357
  2512 Program Drive
  Dallas, Texas 75229
  (214) 357-6494

Budget Films
  4590 Santa Monica Blvd.
  Los Angeles, California 90029
  (213) 660-0187

Cine Craft Company
  1720 N.W. Marshall
  P.O. Box 4126
  Portland, Oregon 97209
  (503) 228-7484

Clem Williams Films, Inc.
  2240 Noblestown Road
  Pittsburgh, Pennsylvania 15205
  (412) 921-5810
  1277 Spring Street, N.W.
  Atlanta, Georgia 30309
  (404) 872-5353
  5424 West North Avenue
  Chicago, Illinois 60639
  (312) 637-3322
  2170 Portsmouth
  Houston, Texas 77006
  (713) 529-3906

Contemporary/McGraw-Hill Films
  Princeton Road
  Hightstown, New Jersey 08520
  (609) 448-1700
  828 Custer Avenue
  Evanston, Illinois 60202
  (312) 869-5010
  1714 Stockton Street
  San Francisco, California 94133
  (415) 362-3115

"The" Film Center
  915 12th Street, N.W.
  Washington, D.C. 20005
  (202) 393-1205

Films Incorporated
  5589 New Peachtree Road
  Atlanta, Georgia 30341
  (404) 451-7445

Deseret Book Co.—Film
  Division
60 East South Temple
Salt Lake City, Utah 84110
(801) 328-8191
161 Massachusetts Avenue
Boston, Massachusetts 02115
(212) 889-7910 (New York)
Knight's Film Library
  (Marine Division)
3911 Normal Avenue
San Diego, California 92103
(714) 298-6163
440 Park Avenue South
New York, New York 10016
(212) 889-7910
5625 Hollywood Blvd.
Hollywood, California 90026
(213) 466-5481
4420 Oakton Street
Skokie, Illinois 60076
(312) 676-1088

Institutional Cinema Service, Inc.
915 Broadway
New York, New York 10010
(212) 673-3990

Ivy Film
165 West 46th Street
New York, New York 10036
(212) 765-3940

National Film Service
14 Glenwood Avenue
Raleigh, North Carolina 27602
(919) 821-0211

Trans-World Films, Inc.
332 South Michigan Avenue
Chicago, Illinois 60604
(312) 922-1530

Twyman Films, Inc.
329 Salem Avenue
Dayton, Ohio 45401
(513) 222-4014

United Artists 16
729 Seventh Avenue
New York, New York 10019
(212) 245-6000

United Films
1425 South Main
Tulsa, Oklahoma 74119
(918) 583-2681

Universal 16
205 Walton Street, N.W.
Atlanta, Georgia 30303
(404) 523-5081

2001 S. Vermont Avenue
Los Angeles, California 90007
(213) 731-2151

425 N. Michigan Avenue
Chicago, Illinois 60611
(312) 822-0513

810 South St. Paul St.
Dallas, Texas 75201
(214) 741-3164

445 Park Avenue
New York, New York 10022
(212) 759-7500

Wholesome Film Center
20 Melrose Street
Boston, Massachusetts 02116
(617) 426-0155

Index

Walden, 97, 103
Walking Tall, 45. *See also* Heroism; Violence
Wallach, Eli, 24
Warshow, Robert, 49, 151
Wayne, David, 73
Wayne, John, 13, 17, 20
Webb, Jack, 3
Widowhood, 85, 89, 93, 96
Wilder, Billy, 2, 6, 7, 8, 10, 12, 80, 137, 138, 151
Williams, Esther, xxiii
Womanhood (women)
  intellectual, 102, 108, 112–17, 119, 127–28;
  minority, 153;
  poor, 153;
  traditional, xiii, xvii–xviii, xx, 16, 34, 35–36, 57, 69–70, 71, 93, 94, 100, 102–3, 118–19, 123, 135–36;
  transitional, xiii, xiv, xvi, xvii,

xx–xxi, xxii, xxiii–xxiv, 8, 16, 17–18, 30–31, 34, 41, 42, 47, 60, 62–63, 69, 71–72, 81, 83, 86, 104, 113, 119–20, 124–25, 136, 150
Woman of the Year, xvi, xviii
Women and Madness, 4
Wood, Natalie, xxiii
Work, xiv, xvi, xvii, 8, 30, 34, 75–76, 77, 85, 130, 153–54
World War II, xvi, xvii, 20, 40, 59, 132, 136
Wright, Teresa, xix
Wyler, William, xix
Wylie, Philip, xvii
Wyman, Jane, 95

Zinnemann, Fred, 48, 49, 52, 56, 124, 125

Out of the quiet 1950s we were cata-
pulted into the feminist revolution of the
1960s. How could it happen so fast?
Were the 1950s really so tranquil?

Brandon French says no. Behind the
obsessive domesticity of the traditional-
ist '50s, she writes, women's demands
were in fact germinating. Evidence of
this is preserved in films of the era, and
the women in them give a clue to the
consciousness of the Americans——men
as well as women——who flocked to see
them.

On the Verge of Revolt affords new
insight into a transitional period that
appeared to be a retreat into idyllic
family-dominated concerns. But that retreat covered up intense cultural denial
for women.

This dislocation of reality from appearance made the '50s, French feels,
the most schizophrenic——and consequently the most misunderstood——
decade of the century. Using astute film
analysis, she deals with the complex effects of an ambiguous female image
on sex, romance, marriage, divorce,
motherhood, ambition, loneliness, alcoholism, heroism, and even the notion of
androgyny. The films examined are:

Sunset Boulevard (1950)
The Quiet Man (1952)
The Marrying Kind (1952)
Shane (1953)
From Here to Eternity (1953)
The Country Girl (1955)
The Tender Trap (1955)
Marty (1955)
All That Heaven Allows (1956)
Picnic (1956)
Heaven Knows, Mr. Allyson (1957)
The Nun's Story (1958)
Some Like It Hot (1959)